Sweet Wonder

Angeline Haen

Sweet Wonder

Angeline Haen

SHANTI ARTS PUBLISHING

BRUNSWICK, MAINE

Published by Shanti Arts Publishing

Designed by Shanti Arts Designs

Cover image: [Santasombra]/stock.adobe.com

Shanti Arts LLC
193 Hillside Road
Brunswick, Maine 04011

shantiarts.com

Printed in the United States of America

ISBN: 978-1-956056-82-2 (softcover)

Library of Congress Control Number: 2023933719

for Wally, I miss you

Contents

Sweet Wonder

Tap Root

Smile Pile

Places to Pause

Give and Thank

Medicine Path

Tiny Teachers

part one

Sweet Wonder

Stone Faced

Do you see it? The smile, the two-finger peace sign? I had forgotten about this little guy. It's no bigger than my thumb-nail. Out of the pouch it tumbled landing face up. Instantly, a feeling of peace and contentment filled my heart. The little stone has a story.

I found this smiley stone over ten years ago on the shores of Big Gitche-Gumee (Lake Superior). I had been trolling the shoreline all day looking for agates. Their beautiful banded patterns formed billions of years ago during lava eruptions. Agates are elusive, often disguised by a rough brownish husk. A full day of agate hunting with nothing to show for my efforts. My enthusiasm was wearing thin.

I found a section of shoreline at the end of a point where the crisp breeze was just strong enough to blow a few pesky black flies out over the lake. Plopping down, I wiggled a bit side-to-side to form a comfy seat in the sun-warmed stones. Forearms resting atop bended knees, I clasped my hands together and hung my head down between my legs. There isn't a plain stone to be seen. All the stones on the shore of Gitche-Gumee have extraordinary beauty, but I so had my heart set on finding a prized agate. Not one to laminate on failure, I soon was fuddling around with the tiny stones where I sat. I liked rubbing the warm smooth surfaces between my fingers. Eyes closed, listening to the waves lapping against the shore. Feeling stones reveals more beauty than eyes can see. That's what I was doing when I found that little stone, feeling its beauty. It was so strong, I picked it up. Bringing the tiny stone within view, I opened my eyes. To my surprise, the little stone was smiling at me and showing me the universal sign for peace. I was speechless. Clasping the stone tight, I held it to my heart, now opened wide and deep. All these years later, I remember how on that day the Universe had different intentions about what I was going to find, and it wasn't going to be what I was looking for.

If I don't find what I am looking for, I like to believe what I do find is looking for me.

Between Skins

Garter Snake left something behind,
a lacy sleeve
of his diamond design.
Soft and fragile,
thin as a whisper.

He breached restriction,
peeled it away.
hooked by the log
inside out and in one piece
the tissue print laid.

Trusting each twist, every turn
Surrendered to the struggle.
I wonder how that feels
to wholly leave behind
all that will not grow with you.

Wet flesh of newborn knowledge
understanding's tender spiral.
Shedding is both
quiet and beautiful,
skin and tears alike.

Garter Snake and I
both have reached this place
where we can be
stretched no further—
stretched no further.

I looked for him
among dead leaves
and smooth grass.
Perhaps he sought refuge
under dark undergrowth.

Restless as the forces of creativity
Garter Snake can't be held still
or tight for long.
When stirred hidden passion glows
like embers buried in ash.

In this place—between skins
all of me
wiggled free
by creative energy.
All of me free.

Here grow the light,
live in the sunfields
when you can be stretched no further
leave something behind—leave something behind.

Sweet Drops

By the shift in the wind's direction and speed, I can tell
the weather is about to change abruptly. The sky's sunny
disposition is no match for the cloud's angry demeanor. As
Wally and I make a bee line for the shelter of the shed, they
come—sweet drops of rest.

I take a seat on an overturned pail near the open
shed door, peering through the curtain of rain. Wally waltzes
over for a scratch behind the ear then lies on my feet. The
distinct odor of wet lab cuts through the scent of fresh rain. I
breathe in both deeply. There we sit, work waiting, listening
to the peaceful rhythm of the rain. Peaceful because there is
no hay ready to bale or seed to put in the ground. Rain and I
have a fluid relationship. To a farmer, rain can be a curse and
a blessing. Weather is a master at teaching acceptance. Over
the years, I've learned to move with the rhythm of the rain.

While thoughts tossing and turning in my mind are
put to sleep by the rain's song, I feel content. We control
uncontrollable circumstances by choosing how we cope with
them. Today I'm choosing to sit and listen to the sweet drops
of wisdom coming to rest in my soul.

Winter Walk

I've returned home from a long walk
in Winter's night
along the woodland's dark edge
a place where shadows play with one's imagination

Peaceful scents of pine escape from emerald green needles
enclosed in the wind's frosty breath
drifting past my rosy running nose
Every last whiff I sniff

Covered by a moonbeam cloak of sequins,
the mesmerizing landscape twinkles in
the mind's wide-open eye

Wakened from a whisper on the wind
forgotten promises remembered
surely Winter, with its pure white heart,
would not be unforgiving.

Clear and cold, attention starved thoughts
want companionship
no turning back now
I follow where they go
down and deep
up and away

Winter nights walk stillness inward
where I hear silence speak
in a soft gray voice
of wonderful things

Wrapped in a hearts warmth, cozy and comfortable
with myself
I let it lead me home sweet home

Shady People

Not everything can live in the sunshine. On my early morning walk with Wally through our little woods, I noticed how happy the trillium and violets were blooming in the shade. Even the fanned-out ferns, which don't really bloom, were content with their place in this world dappled with light. They made me think of the shady people in my life. How, in the presence of other people's brightness, they burn. But in the shadows, they shine; their living light a reflection of this calm . . . cool . . . collected energy.

I appreciate the different sensitivities in our personalities. It's not so much that their beauty is hidden, but unseen. We have to enter the shadows to fully understand them—something not all of us are willing to do. Most shady people I know are introverted and extremely creative. I can only imagine the brilliance of the inner light that sources their visions. Sadly, it is a light some can struggle to find. Sunshine and darkness can be equally blinding. That's when the compass of our higher self gives us direction, points us to that feeling of center within us. The place that keeps the light on.

We all thrive where we feel alive. I love my shady friends. Not everyone can live in the sunshine. Some people are made for the shade.

Dark's Secret Haiku

Night bleeds from day's break
Brilliant color stains the sky
Darkness keeps secrets

Holy Harmony

What ear doesn't turn toward the winged-one's song
thick in the March air?
Passionate chords strung together on heart strings,
hoping to snare a mate.

On a limb touching the sky I see him.
His crisp crimson outline easy to spot against the
drab scenery.

His whole body reverberates the rapture in each note.
Following the rhythm of nature's pounding chest.
I pause. Such intensity.

I wonder, could it be a primordial song of survival?
I feel the lifeless unborn come alive.
His voice drowning in anticipation of a response.

Who doesn't hear the song's holy harmony?
The loud thrumming of his calls pierce the silence.
The heart's winter sleeps no more!

Songs Pray

Dew holds tight to the bushes and berries
Its grip loosened by the soft caress of dry cloth
Mornings these days are early and damp.

Flower faces reflect the sun's smile
Standing tall above them all
a perfectly pink Phlox bloom
I pause to savor the sniff
Heaven dreams of a smell so sweet

In the patch worry rests
You can hear songs
Ancestral songs
The kind that come on their own
The kind that sing themselves
The kind that pray

Hollow bones hold the songs
I sing the praises of mobility and ruby red raspberries
Oh, the voice may crack and pop
But it carries the tune well enough

Handfuls of delight dangle from the tips of grateful fingers
I'll harvest all I can from this juicy life
Fill my bucket and then some
Before I'm dead ripe

The Salesman

> "The soil is the great connector of lives, the source
> and destination of all. It is the healer and restorer and
> resurrector, by which disease passes into health, age into
> youth, death into life. Without proper care for it we can
> have no community, because without proper care for it we
> can have no life."
>
> —Wendell Berry, *The Unsettling of America:*
> *Culture and Agriculture*

I became acquainted with Robert during my search for an
affordable alternative to agricultural lime. Soil tests the
previous year revealed that most of the ground our hay
fields grew on had turned sour. Their PH levels were under
7. Calcium is what you apply to raise the soil's PH level. It
was the cause of our dwindling harvests. If you are a wise
farmer, you understand the sacredness of your relationship with soil and do all you can to promote, preserve, and
protect a healthy soil environment.

Robert worked for a company that sold liquid
calcium. Liquid calcium had many advantages over dry lime,
but I had never used it before. I had questions. Lots of them.
I needed to educate myself on the product. After receiving
Robert's initial response to an email, I could tell he was a
salesman through and through. The email was pages of
information and customer testimonials singing the praises
of his product. As I sifted through the information, I had to
wonder—was it all smoke and mirrors? Or was his perceived
confidence trusted truth?

Then the phone call happened. His sentences strung
together like a fine pearl necklace. I could tell the sales
pitch had been recited hundreds, if not thousands of time,
locked in his memory from the repetition. He drew out

the vowels of his words in typical southern drawl fashion. By its tone and fluctuations, I guessed he was close to retirement. Here and there his words slurred together into unintelligible sentences. Even so, it was a pleasant voice to listen to. That was fortunate because Robert did most of the talking. True to his old school sales techniques, he peppered the conversation with sweetheart bombs and young lady references. I didn't mind. They lightened the scientific nature of the conversation and ever so gently tickled my heart. Occasionally, to make sure I was still a captive audience, there would be a quick, "You follow me, dear?" He had me smiling at the first sweetheart.

Robert's inquisitive questions about our fertilizer needs gradually turned to the joys and tribulations that come with living close to the land. The topic ranged from bringing in a bumper crop of hay to the weather here in Wisconsin and the rising price of everything. We lamented briefly about getting older. More questions came when we realized we shared a fondness for horses. How long had I had the horses? What were their names? Did I ride often? They began to reflect a genuine concern for the land and the people who tend to it. I didn't feel any pressure. I wasn't wasting any of Robert's time whether he got the sale or not.

Near the end of the conversation I learned that Robert was seventy-three years old with no plans to retire any time soon. At the conclusion of the call, I was reading off my credit card number. My encounter with Robert brought to mind a quote by Theodore Roosevelt: "People don't care how much you know until they know how much you care."

Lost in the Shadows

through the night's darkness
an icy mist fell
fog floats over the earth
like a gray phantom

nothing left untouched
dampness drips from the landscape's heavy bones

a mystical mist
mother earth's breath
trapped in the fallen sky
silently heaven's soft kiss moves in

sunrise sweet lips
a gentle warmth reached

chill crumbles in the face of light
numbed emotions thaw
mysterious meanings revealed

I walk with my feelings
toward light's waiting kiss
behind me
lost in the shadows
my darkness

Manure Meditations

Caring for farm animals means you are stuck in a perpetual poop cycle. For the most part, what goes in one end comes out the other. I've done my share of pitching and piling in this life. The tedious task effortlessly takes my quieted mind into a manure meditation.

We don't give a second thought to the negative connotations we associate with various expressions for crap, but I hope I can make you question that perception. After much poop pondering, I now look at the mound of manure accumulated over the long winter and see it as a pile of potential. Once composted, the nutrient rich organic matter will be worth more to me than money in the bank.

In nature there is no want beyond what is needed. Nothing is wasted. In one way or another, the sustenance taken from the earth is eventually returned to her. Single stream recycling at its finest. I doubt Creator wants us to feel or think any part of our life is wasted either. Those less than desirable experiences have value. If we do the dirty work of decomposing the drama, we enrich our understanding on how to transform the trauma. It's a way to build long-term emotional resiliency, to understand those deep-rooted feelings that no longer serve our highest good. We want next season's seeds to fall on good ground.

Through the process of integration (composting), we gain a wealth of meaning from the negativity coming into our life. It's how we grow our soul—not away, but from those experiences that have depleted us. Rich fertile soul soil to cultivate a positive perspective.

In a manner of speaking, it matters how you look at sh*t.

I Watched

I watched you in silence.
Right there, a few feet in front of me,
hunkered next to a fading violet plant,
frantically scratching at the ground beneath it.

I watched the violet reluctant to release the earth's clasp
in its roots,
exposed and vulnerable, surrender inevitable.
Sharp teeth penetrate the tender white skin with ease.

I watched intently as you nibbled off tiny pieces.
Sickle-shaped claws pushing, pushing,
forcing a place for another tiny bit, then another and another.
Was there no end to Chipmunk cheek capacity?
I watched you scamper off into the nearby woods.

I watch and learn
I am a student
I am being watched
I am a teacher.

Observer and observed,
silent watching.
I wonder what am I teaching?
I will have to wait and watch.

Saints and Angels

Little did I expect that a slight deviation from my usual route home would have me wrestling with a saint and hitching a ride with two angels!

The distant horizon sizzles with hues of orange and yellow as the sun burns down for the day. My five-dollar sunglasses do nothing to relieve the discomfort, so I resort to looking through the slits of my lowered eyelids. Further on, I vaguely make out a four-legged animal crisscrossing the road. As the distance diminishes, I see a large St. Bernard dog. Oblivious to the angry honks and near misses of passing cars, the saint seems to have a guardian angel sitting on his shoulder. I decide that taking the saint out of harm's way will be worth the slight interruption to my commute home.

I pull over onto the road's gravel shoulder. Half my car still protrudes into the lane of traffic. In the dwindling light, the glow of my car's yellow hazard lights provides intermittent protection as cars zip by.

His nose hovers just a fraction of an inch above the earth, inhaling the sweet essence of virgin ground. The saint doesn't even notice me. I tap my hands on both knees and, in a high-pitched, soft mothering tone, I call out, "Come here, boy! Come here! Aren't you a handsome fellow?" Not even a glimpse my way. It didn't take long for me to realize that I was no match for the sights and smells of the impending adventure of unfettered canine freedom. Hmm. What to do? I return to my car and take the ten-minute-old sub out and, like magic, I have the saint's attention!

The saint lumbers over to me. Grabbing his collar is the easy part, reading his tag proved to be as infuriating as the buzz of a mosquito when you're trying to fall asleep.

A phone number is printed on the tab. Sub devoured, he wants to go where he wants to go. I see Wally's leash. With a Houdini-like maneuver, I manage to get the leash snapped onto his collar. I take out my phone and call the number on the collar. It's a veterinary office. The secretary has no luck contacting the owner, so she gives me the saint's home address. I decide the easiest option is to simply take him home.

After several long minutes of trying to coerce the stubborn saint into the back of my car, it's obvious he doesn't want to get in a vehicle, much less ride in one. *OK*, I say under my breath. *I'll just walk you home.* By my best guesstimate, I figure his rural route address is east of our present location.

After a few steps, I realize our fate is sealed. The adventure begins. His familiarity of being led on leash is even less than that of his time riding in a vehicle. He proceeds to drag me in and out of the ditch at will. I get soaked on the first ditch detour, but I'm not letting go. Stiff, dry weed stalks are cutting my arms. At points, he lies down and refuses to move. After catching his breath, he's off and running. I brace myself against mailboxes to keep us from heading into traffic. I am as determined to hang on as he is to make me let go! My breath is heavy and hot, the salty taste of sweat on my lips. We tangle and untangle in the cord tethering us together like a choreographed dance between capture and escape.

Finally, as the glow of the sun's dying embers burns out, I find his house. My guesstimate was terribly wrong. After heading a quarter-mile east, we had to double back and go another quarter-mile west. Of course, nobody is home, so I confine him to the garage. Satisfied my punishing ordeal is over, I give myself a once over. Mud covers my numb arms, and the constant jerking motion has given me a sore shoulder. Beneath the cool mud balm, the sting of tiny cuts and scrapes works its way through the dried blood.

I am a hot mess. I mean that literally, not figuratively. As I shake my head in disbelief, giggles wiggle out. The giggle quickly turns to hysterical laughter. I tuck knotted strands of hair riddled with weeds behind my ear. As I struggle to regain my composure, far in the distance, I see the faint pulsing glow of yellow hazard lights. The good laugh seems to have been the perfect balm for all my wounds. Satisfied my saintly mission is accomplished, I head out carrying its good medicine—laughter.

Exhaustion is setting in and each step is heavy and slow. The smile still stretched across my face, I ask my guardian angels for protection and strength as I walk down the silent country road, the gleam of headlights gone. With a chuckle, I say out loud, *I guess you never know where a good deed will "lead"...you...Angie.*

Then out of nowhere, a car appears! The arm of its passenger frantically waving me over. I can't believe it! Two wonderful women offer me a ride back to my car. As we drive, I recount the St. Bernard story to rousing laughter. Laughter has a way of lifting the weight of our humanness off our spirits. As we depart, I have an amusing thought. Not all saints are angels!

"So shines a good deed in a weary world."
—Willy Wonka

Sacred Space

Betweenness brings a notion of imbalance, but to me it's the imbalance that brings us into these seams of life to sew the separated pieces together. Betweenness frees us from being stuck in a relationship, job, indecision, etc. The hard places of betweenness is where we are given the opportunity to view both sides of our circumstances. We come into difficult places of uncertainty to thread softness into our judgments and beliefs about ourselves.

Betweens are a threshold to a spiritual state of contemplation, a place of gentle unfolding to be still and listen for guidance in order to take the right next action. You're stuck for a reason. The fray of betweenness is where opening to our higher self begins. These are powerful places where we are able to observe and understand how we got where we are, so we can get where we want to go. We forget how much of life is lived in this potent space for intuitive decision making. The pause between our breaths, words, thoughts; these are sacred spaces charged with clarity.

In the realm of divine mystery, living from one's heart center can be a struggle. In-between times awaken the heart's center, bringing us especially close to Spirit. When we can connect to true center—our heart—we immediately come into balance. Wrinkles of doubt get ironed out. The posture of our relatedness to any situation we happen to be experiencing is brought into perspective. Choices can have a raw edge. With a balanced view we are able to see things as they are, hem in the worry, and life stops unraveling.

part two

Tap Root

Recipes for Love

Every holiday I find myself seated at the kitchen table with a cup of coffee, sifting through a drawer of recipes. The search is as much for family recipes as it is for memories. It doesn't take long before I find them both.

Before my mom and aunties passed, they gifted me a few of their kitchen secrets and well-used kitchen items. There's Busha's (Grandma's) hand-forged, three-pronged fork. The stubby handle fits perfectly in the palm of a hand when cutting in shortening. Busha cooked on a woodstove. Every meal was a laborious and monumental task. I don't think the stove was ever cold to the touch.

I treasure Mom's solid wood rolling pin and flour sack towels. Mom always rolled out her dough on a well-floured flour sack. Thin from two generations of washings, I handle them with extreme care and use them exclusively for rolling out dough.

To find one of Mom's recipes with conventional measurement is not the norm. Her measurements were by feel or taste. It's probably why Mom would call me to come over and "watch" her make something. She would often tell me, "I'm not going to live forever. If you want to learn how to make this, keep watching." I'm glad I did so her love can nourish the next generation.

There's Auntie Anna's substantially cracked and chipped blue speckled enamelware pan. It must have been a favorite based on its condition. I'm so happy she held on to it and passed it on to me. Believe it or not—nothing ever sticks to that pan! Auntie Anna's cooking instructions were loud, clear, and concise. Her stern direction carried over from her many years running the kitchen for the local church's annual picnic.

Then there's Auntie Rosie's titanic-sized cast iron frying pan. In her later years, arthritis prevented her from lifting the heavy weight. The pan than became a permanent fixture on her stovetop. Cleanup was a wipe or two with a paper towel. Still is.

I can't forget Auntie Vickey's delectable dessert recipes. The handwritten recipes have yellowed with age. Torn edges of the fragile paper have been taped together several times. The tape too has yellowed. A busy farmer's wife, Auntie Vickey's countertops and kitchen table held much of the overflow from her cupboards. She could make a meal fit for king in minutes!

If you haven't guessed, I am descended from a long line of amazing Polish women who knew their way around a kitchen. Once I was old enough to hold a wooden spoon in my hand, they pressed me into service at some task that was age-appropriate. Any family gathering, no matter how large or small, ended with a meal. Crumbs on the table were never casually wiped to the floor. Licked fingers firmly pressed the bits against the tabletop. The finger with moist crumbs attached was promptly licked clean. Every last crumb of life's deliciousness was savored.

The strong Polish women in my life grew up in a generation that didn't say "I love you" out loud very often, if ever. Words of love may not have been shared but they did share recipes to taste it. What else could be created in the heart of the home—the kitchen—but love?

Busha

A continuous cloud of dust followed our truck up the driveway that spilled into Busha's yard. Mom was the first out. My sister and I usually hesitated—with good reason. Busha kept a flock of geese. They would stay out of sight, but their menacing honking and hissing echoed behind every rickety outbuilding. We would only make the mad dash to the front door when assured that the skin on the backs of our necks would not be pinched by their vise grip beaks.

The poured concrete steps leading into her home were pitted and chipped, slightly tilted toward the home's foundation, and not nearly adequate when it came to their width. Where the sharp corners of the door trim met the frame, about waist high, a palm-wide patch of wood was rounded smooth from years of use as a handrail. Although the door hung straight, it took several pulls before its stubbornness would give way.

The air in the entryway was dank and musty, used mostly to keep several cords of firewood dry and close at hand to feed the wood-burning cookstove. By the time you made it up the few steps that led to the kitchen, Busha's smile could be seen peering through the open door, her knee-length hair up in a tidy bun, hands excitedly wringing the front of her apron, and an animated Polish greeting urging you to come and sit at the small table positioned under the single window that lit the room.

These are among the few memories I have of my maternal grandmother. Sometimes it's not how much you know about a person but what you know of them that matters.

Call of the Land

Wisps of earth perfumed the air. The scent of fresh, moist soil drifted through a maze of barn odors to be within sniffing distance of my nose. The whiff tickled the air, making my nose crinkle. I drew in a long, full, deliberate breath. Dad was plowing the side field and the land was calling me to play in a whisper of a whisper on the air.

I can't recollect how long I had been standing in the doorway of the barn, that betwixt and between place where the inside air that was thick with odors of cattle, feed, and manure mingled with the outside air that was crisp, fresh, and inviting. I was taking a break from the lingering morning chores, graining the milk cows, feeding the calves, and washing up the milking equipment. Dad left me to finish up as he was anxious to begin plowing. Washing the milking equipment was always left for last. I wouldn't go so far as to say I hated the milk house clean-up, but it earned a position at the bottom of my "to do" list anyway. I always felt a great sense of accomplishment when I stood back admiring the gleaming stainless-steel hanging from the walls. That felt good. The dislike came from what didn't feel good—what it took to get it that way. The pungent detergents bit at your skin and burned your nostrils as it purged the remnants of milk and grime from a menagerie of hoses and containers. The bulk tank was deep and reaching in the sides cut into my armpits being I was short on one end. Scrubbing was occasionally a necessity when the milk dried and bound to the rubber of the teat cups with the tenacity of a junk yard dog chewing a bone. This was usually caused when washing the milking equipment moved from beyond 'last' on my chore list to 'forgotten'.

The bristles of farm chores never brushed down to

actual work in my mind. I took joy and gave delight in each menial task. Farming offered a life of consistency, freedom, risk, uncertainty and pride in what two hands, a strong back and a willing mind could accomplish if they worked in harmony with the land, answered her call. Back then, if you were a farmer, it was because you loved the land. You were called by the land to steward the bountiful abundance of love and life that emanated from each stitch in the patch you were fortunate enough to care for.

To me being called a farm girl was a compliment of the highest accord. Being raised on a farm was like receiving a kiss from God, pressed on the hand of fate, lovingly blown to me by destiny. I knew a few other farm girls from school that thought otherwise. They were of the opinion that being raised on a farm was a cruel fate, robbing them of their dignity and Palmolive soft hands.

I steered clear of the house as much as possible. It was my mother's domain. The only place I felt controlled, confined. The house was for eating, sleeping and forced cleaning of both it and myself. The only miserable thought I had during this time of year, spring, was the increased frequency in which the cleaning of both the house and I had to be performed. You weren't a farm kid if you didn't have dirt under your fingernails, bruised skinned knees and semi-permanent dirt ring around the soles of your feet. Bath time provided an opportunity for the soap and water to attempt the removal of the dirt and crud lodged within the crevices, crinkles and wrinkles of my tough weather worn skin. It wasn't very successful most of the time even if I soaked in it until the skin on my fingers resembled that of a prune, an over cooked one at that.

In the distance, I could hear the hum of the tractor engine. A 1555 Oliver, bought brand spanking new in the seventies. She was at full throttle making good time turning the soil to its side. Every so often I knew when Dad had circled back to the low end of the field because I could hear her bog down and give out a growl, straining under the pull of the wet heavy soil that wasn't ready to be broken from its hold on sleep. Plowing was truly an awakening of the land, drawing the covers from her face after a long winters sleep. The earth was coming alive, renewing the gifts only she was capable of giving, the gifts of sustained life from her fertile womb.

Finally, the cows finished licking up the last morsels of their sweet ground feed. It was time to let them out to pasture. Soon the clink of opening and closing snaps was echoing through the manger. I'd hang each chain neatly over the stall head ready to accept the cows for evening milking in an efficient manner. As they walked through the gateway the land once again called to me in the wind. Eager to assess Dad's progress, I climbed the gate to see what portion of land was painted with the rich hues of brown and gold that only the brush held in the hand of a plow can paint. Seeing that most of the canvas remained blank I decided I would ride the Oliver for a bit until a substantial amount of ground lay waiting for my amusement, a real playground.

I gave one last pat to the back side of Spunker, the matriarch of the herd, the aluminum gate shut behind her with clank, narrowly missing her hind hock. She was old, wise and a putz, pretty much held the attitude that she had nothing to do and all day to do it. She was born on the farm and my favorite because of her unusual markings. Spunker had a white line down the length of her back and a speckle black and white face. Her body was black except for a white bullseye on her butt and white socks. I helped bring her into the world and she helped me be in this world.

Off I ran, taking the short cut under the electric fence, through the cow pasture and over the ditch. Crossing the cow pasture, I had to be mindful and aware of each well-placed step since I was barefoot and it was laden with fresh cow pies as the cows swaggered to the far end of the pasture. I remember one time when I dashed to head off a heifer, Little Blue that was reluctant to come into the corral. I felt a warm soft ooze flow between each toe of my left foot as I planted it to make a quick change of direction to cut her off. It wasn't that I was grossed out by the fact I'd just stepped into a pile of shit; it was the "eww" feeling that caused my disgust. I promptly perused my surroundings looking for a solution, only to see grass bitten down to bare ground, much too short to pass between toes. Luckily, I spied a lush patch of White Dutch clover nearby and I was able to wipe a majority of the slice of cow pie from the bottom and sides of my feet. It was between my toes that caused the dilemma. I began to methodically separate each toe from the one next to it and brush my foot, this way and that way, through the clover blossoms. I was very pleased with the outcome. I walked proudly behind Little Blue into the barn and down the main aisle with a sweet-scented clover blossom between each toe of my left foot.

I opted to intersect the Oliver at the closest point to the pasture fence, it was an unspoken knowing that when I made my way toward the Oliver, I was coming with something or nothing on my mind. Today it was nothing. I made my way to the end of the field near a newly laid furrow and waited for the Oliver and Dad to round the corner. Dad eased the Oliver to a stop and I began the labored rise to my perch on the fender. Sometimes Dad would make like he was coming at me with the tractor and pretend to swerve the steering wheel toward me. He'd flick the ashes from his

Marlboro and flash me a smile. The tractor was at a peculiar angle when plowing, as the set of wheels on one side followed without protest the open furrow, while the other set rode on untouched ground. The Oliver and plow would lose their equilibrium on each turn into the new furrow, wobbling and swaying briefly on the uneven ground until the turn was completed and the peculiar angle was once again sustained. This made standing the most tolerable position when plowing and the one I would choose today.

There was a strategically placed handle welded onto the fender, but when standing I mostly relied on Dad's shoulder. When I was much younger, four or five years old, Dad would squeeze me between him and the steering wheel, managing to give me an inch or so of the seat, all a youngster needs for comfort. That gave me great delight because when the way was straight and clear, I took over the wheel, standing with an outstretched neck struggling to see over the tractor's mountainous frame.

I since outgrown the privileged position and made do the best I could. The knobby knees of an eight-year-old served only to be in the way when riding the Oliver. By the end of summer, they would be decorated with black and blue medals, somewhat round configurations that blended nicely with the tones of red displayed in the back drop of scrape cover my skin. I could tell you with precise detail, who, what, when, where, and how I had the misfortune to receive every last one of the scrapes and bruises because each one had a story to tell about me. The stories were rekindled in an instant if you made the slightest glance or comment about the way my knees looked. You would then be subjected to a flawless rendition of each and every last story, embellished with facial expressions and full body dramatics. The bruises came from the constant knocking of my knees against a myriad of levers, controllers, and doohickeys that maneuvered the equipment like a robotic extension of Dad's arm.

The Oliver's engine hummed a soothing song and my senses soon numbed. A trance-like state floated over and within me as I watched the rows of ground turning over each other, again, and again, and again. My eyelids would feel the heaviness of the morning's work, and my tired legs would begin to give at the knees, jerking me from my doziness for a brief sudden moment. When I started to drift to sleep the ride was over. It was simply too dangerous and Dad eased the Oliver's engine down once again, and I began a sluggish decent to the earth.

The Oliver 1555 tractor is still running well and working the land as it has for the past fifty years. Three generations have sat behind the wheel. I feel Dad's smile from heaven every time I turn the key. When I sit in her cracked worn seat and tenderly slide my hand around the steering wheel, I drift back to a time when the voice of your character was spoken in the life you led; back then you stood on your reputation, built it on integrity with a foundation of hard work.

It was time to play! The land was my playground, a natural wonder emporium, overflowing with adventure and brimming with exploration. I was always in awe when seemingly out of nowhere flocks of seagulls would begin to appear whenever Dad plowed. There angelic white bodies drew stark contrast against the dark shadowy soil. It wasn't that we lived particularly close to water, but the Bay of Green Bay was a ten-minute ride as the crow flies. I just figured they heard the call of the land in a whisper of a whisper on the air. They feasted on the plump, dazed grubs riddling the surface of the ground. I'd lie still as a statue taking in their beauty then suddenly rise and run toward the flock startling them into taking flight like clouds returning to the sky.

The plowed ground exposed all kinds of buried treasures, magnificently colored stones of every size shape. Ancient stone people at rest for eons now arisen. It would take centuries but the elements would return them again to what they once were. Rusted memories of long forgotten machinery pieces lay in their earthen graves without markers. The apex of treasures for me…a horseshoe. I was horse crazy and finding a horse shoe was like receiving a sign, a message from God that I was a pinch closer to waking from my dream of having a horse. Over the years, I found five horseshoes. They hang in the home I occupy today. They serve as a wonderful reminder of how lucky I was to be raised on a farm and to have a horse share my journey through the winding trails of childhood.

I'd stroke and dig at the furrows, breaking away roots holding to life with a death grip. I'd weave the long hairy strands into jewelry and adorn my wrists and head with the twisted intricate embellishments. Lots of creepy crawlies lived among them too, fascinating creatures that wiggled and squirmed about when they no longer felt the Earth beneath them. I do the same when I distance myself from the land, go too far away to hear her call, I become uneasy and restless. What joy I found in finding a friend that was so small and squirmy.

Walking across the lay of the furrow was difficult. When you followed the furrow there was buoyancy to each step, a slight spring that loped you forward. This was good fodder for fantastic imaginary games I'd play in my head. My active imagination gained momentum and fueled my legs and spirit as I ran across the field, blurring the lines of reality and make believe. I'm sure I was quite the sight, flapping my fully extended arms as if I would take flight every bellow from arm wings - in my mind I already had.

Everything in nature intrigued me, especially animals. I liked to think of my imagination as animal-aided, instead of animated, although, the meaning was the same, so many vivid exchanges of pure joy and spontaneous laughter. It matters not if they were real or imagined only that I made myself believe, playing makes you believe. This taught me that you have to believe in something for it to become anything, and if that something you believe in is your imagination, dreams come true.

By now my tummy was rumbling and as I looked up, squinting, I could see the sun had raised high in the sky; Dad had finished plowing and was heading the Oliver toward the yard. His tummy must have been rumbling too, as much as I wanted to stay, I begrudgingly moved in the direction of the house. The land would still be there after breakfast. It would be there for me my entire life.

I was baptized a child of the Earth by no other means than being birthed a farmer's daughter, growing up on the nourishing bosom of nature, tasting the sweetness of life in the land of milk and honey. Mother Earth bore me, Mother Nature raised me. There are no ornate ceremonies honoring the sacrament. It's a calling to communion with the land, a primal ache to be so intimate with the Earth that you feel the rhythm of her heart pulsating through the blood in your veins. Age and experience have whittled away at my doubts of connection with her like a sharp knife to soft poplar. I am evolving from hearing the call of the land to listening to her voice echoing in my heart and guiding my actions, a call to teach our children to honor and respect her gifts of transformation, healing medicine power, and messages of wisdom. In simple words, do more to heal than harm her, so our children's children will recognize her voice when they hear the call echo in their hearts.

Positive Propagation

The woods are slow to fill up with snow and cold this winter. I have yet to wear more than one layer of wool when walking Wally. Old Man Winter's unpredictable emotions keep me wary. The snow shovel and extra woollies will be kept within reach.

Unable to enjoy the usual playful snow activities has left a void in this winter. Then with impeccable timing they come! Slow at first. Soon opening the mailbox needs to be done with great care or an avalanche of shiny, slippery catalogs slides to the ground.

One staple I can always count on to brighten a winter day is currently piling up on my kitchen counter. I save them for those especially long and dreary days—seed catalogs! They come at a time when forgiveness for last year's garden disappointments is easy to offer up. I'm ready for another go at the garden's blank canvas.

I have my favorites, the tried and true. Oh, but on the next catalog page I'm tempted to believe the "too good to be true." The colorful photos and persuasively written descriptions fill me with anticipation. Small seeds of optimism take hold with a promise to grow.

Life is like a mailbox full of seed catalogs. You never know how much beauty you can grow until you plant it.

Seed Catalog

Spring seed catalogs
loyal as my old dog
piled up on the table
a late winter mailbox staple.

Slippery glossy pages for some
no frills no fancy for others
black ink on plain paper
for this one.

New and improved promises to create
bountiful blooms on the garden's clean slate
last year's disappointments easily forgiven
with one glance to the next page
I escape from winter's white prison.

Favorite varieties come first
the tried and true-blue
but then there are the new
that make you utter, "Oooo"!
Could they be too good to be true?

Colorful descriptions shout
no pest no drought will kill you out
this one will grow anywhere
without a doubt!

In deep winter optimism can be hard to muster
these light moments keep their luster
dog-eared pages mark the best
scorn the limits on the sum to invest!

Elderberry Gifts

As I pick, the prominent creases in my palms fill with the deep purple, almost black juice of the elderberries. The plastic fork I use to comb the berries from the stems jabs and pokes the delicate skin, bursting the deepest flavored berries. I decide to use my fingers to coerce the berries from their stems—an effort to save as much of the precious juice as possible for the medicinal concoction I'll be making. I relish the intimate hand labor to collect sustenance for my body. Ray Bradbury said it best when he described the art of doing things by hand as something that imbues actions with spirit and enduring significance.

Several years ago, I discovered an enviable passion for the medicinal properties of elderberries. Elderberry's antioxidant capacity is one of the highest of all wild food sources. A tablespoon a day of elderberry syrup is enough to stave off the most arduous cold and flu season. As with many things, homemade is not only better but cheaper. So, fifteen years ago, along a shallow ditch next to a wild space, I planted ten elderberry whips, a florescent ribbon marking their place in the wilderness. All I could do was let time pass.

The head-high bushes started producing at ten years. Most harvests now produce enough to share with friends, family, and a variety of bird species. The birds have spread the seeds by a method I lightheartedly refer to as "poop and plant." Our property now has scatterings of elderberry bushes that are exclusively food for wildlife. The serendipitous way that "passing it forward" occurred makes me wonder if nature had a plan for my relationship with the elderberry all along. The land has been waiting to welcome the elderberry. Evidenced by its proliferation into the hidden wild areas that only a winged-one can reach.

With that thought, I would like to share my elderberry syrup recipe. I'm not really sure you can call it a recipe; it's more of a creative adventure in food preservation. I hope that during the process you feel the hand/heart connection and that your being is imbued with spirit, knowing the enduring significance this one action has on the health and well-being of all that surrounds you.

Elderberry Syrup

Ingredients: elderberry juice (2–3 cups), 1 tsp cinnamon, 3/4 tsp ginger, raw honey

Put clean elderberries into a pot with a good splash of water. Whatever you pick will be enough. Bring to a boil, then turn down to a simmer. Crush berries in the pot. Let them cook at a simmer, crushing and mixing, for 5–10 minutes. A potato masher works well. Once you feel you have squeezed every last drop of juice from the berries, drain the liquid. I use a mesh strainer. To the liquid add the spices. Adjust amounts to your taste. The measurements I give are a starting point. Add the raw honey after the juice has cooled. Stir well. SYRUP MUST BE STORED IN THE REFRIGERATOR.

I take a tablespoon a day beginning in September. It's yummy drizzled over yogurt or mixed into oatmeal.

Barn Raised

The weathered gray skeleton stood proud against the farm country's bluebird sky. The iconic, brilliant, barn-red painted boards stripped nearly bare of color by the hands of time. The crumbling fieldstone foundation slowly being consumed by a Virginia creeper vine, a lone piece of rusted bent tin on the roof flapping in the wind like a lover's perfunctory wave goodbye. The barn's door left open for a generation, hangs by a single hinge at the top. I love the stories old barns tell. They hold on to their majestic beauty and charm to the bitter end. Age comes to them with dignity and pride.

I can say with pride and privilege that I was barn raised. Growing up on a dairy farm means half your childhood is spent in a barn. Created inside a barn is a world of its own making. You sense the unity of family, the separation of seasons, and the guidance of spirituality, a universe of swirling scents punctuated by the sharp freshness of clear thoughts. Chores become a meditation.

The rich textures of rural life are vanishing along with the old wooden barns. Farming and barns have evolved with technological advances. There is a haunting sadness that one day they will all disappear, taking their sacred stories with them. Oh, how I wish barn boards could not only talk but write.

The barn of my childhood has been repurposed several times and its breath no longer smells of those scents from a past I remember, when cows called the stalls home and playful bawls of calves echoed through the center aisle. Still, the feeling of protection and shelter lingers. Being barn raised built my body timber strong, taught me family included the livestock, the weather, the soil, and the seed. The old barn was my church, my dance hall, and my sanctuary. You can take the girl off the farm, but you can't take the farm out of her blood or the barn out of a heart.

"Man, despite his artistic pretensions, his sophistication and many accomplishments, owes the fact of his existence to a six-inch layer of topsoil and the fact that it rains."

—John Jeavons

Seed Haiku

Small seeds of sweetness
Push through the hardness of life
Proliferate love

Collapsed Crib

It was harvest time on our farm, time to reap what we had sown throughout the year, which was mainly our corn crop. The corn's rite of passage from field to feed went through a series of boisterous machines. Each machine link tugged at the corn's tan-painted husks, ripping the leathery petals into shredded fragments. The sun-bleached, pale white husks seemed to come off more easily. Then there were those husks that peeled back around the full circumference of the cob, forming a stiff skirt with a pointed hem at the cob's base. Freed husks flirted with the bashful blue sky, flying up and up, exposing naked kernels to be polished by the sun's breath. The excitement of the harvest made me pop with effervescent joy.

After being run through the corn picker and up the conveyor, the corn went into a corncrib. Every farm had one or two of them when I was growing up. The older style was rectangular in shape with timber frames supporting stiff hardware wire around the sides. The cribs were set on cinder blocks that allowed the wind to move beneath the bounty of corn. Airflow was necessary for newly harvested corn so it would dry and not spoil; without it, the crop decayed. This airflow was enhanced as corn was removed from the cribs on a routine basis. Thus was the honor of safeguarding the harvest bestowed on this humble structure. The golden harvest was protected within its wire belly.

Holding on to an old harvest isn't a good practice, for mildew and mold grow plentifully on aging cobs that are past their prime. Spoilage can move through a dormant crib with the speed of water running downhill.

Dad's relief always showed in his smile when the last shovelful of corn was emptied from the crib with plenty of time to spare before the new crop arrived. With the crib empty, a thorough inspection and assessment of maintenance needs would then be performed. There is a necessary openness to emptiness, a space for hope, faith, and trust to be replenished, restored, and renewed. An opening to do maintenance.

In the winter of my thirteenth year, I witnessed our corncrib fall from grace, succumbing to abundance's burden. Years would pass before I would entirely understand this lesson in harvest hoarding.

Successive years of an abundant crop meant our crib never emptied. Every available storage space held corn. No one needed corn and the prices fell. New corn piled on top of old corn. The crib went without its usual precrop inspection for several seasons. This meant the weakened planks on the crib floor were hidden from sight and overlooked. In life, without a solid floor of values beneath you, you set yourself up for collapse. Being empty makes room for something new to come in.

As it happened, the physical collapse of our corncrib floor went unnoticed for many months. From what we could see from the outside, all seemed well. Then, as winter bore down on the farm, a messenger came announcing the dreadful news that manifested in the form of a medium-sized, snake-tailed rodent. I was the first to see its shadow porpoise across the barn aisle before it escaped my scrutiny by hiding in the safe haven provided by a stack of neatly piled hay. I stood momentarily in disbelief. Fetching a flashlight, I snuck in closer to get a better look. As I squinted into the narrow dark tunnels between the bales, my eyes suddenly saw his gleaming beady eyes looking right back at me. A fear-filled, high-pitched sound escaped my clenched teeth. Robotically, my shoulders squeezed inward, arms crossed tight, hugging my ribs. Sure enough, it WAS a R-A-T!

In the midthirties, when my father was in his twenties, he was employed at the Union Stock Yard in Chicago. He once told me it got so that he could eat his lunch sitting on a dead cow. You lived and worked among rats at that time and in that place. It was at the stock yard that I believe Dad crystallized his hatred for rats.

On our farm, with the arrival of our new guest and with the fire of abhorrence burning hot, Dad immediately devised a plan to eliminate the rat. Where had the rat come from? How long had it been here? Were there more of its kind?

Soon after, what we thought was the lone rat was found in one of the traps Dad set along the barn wall. But mysterious mounds of brown earth began appearing around the snow-packed base of the corncrib. Dad and I went to investigate. With a little poking and prodding, two things became painfully obvious: Several boards in the floor of the corncrib had busted under the weight of the corn, and the population of rats inhabiting the wire fortress was far greater than one. Added to that, there was enough corn to feed the rat kingdom well through winter.

During that winter and early spring, Dad would take potshots at the rats with his .22 as they ventured farther away from the overrun accommodations underneath the corncrib. We contemplated how to get rid of them, and although poison was the obvious choice, it was not the first or best one. The invisible effects of poisons are far-reaching, and we were wary of going that route. However, nothing but complete eradication was acceptable to Dad. For now, the rats were winning and we were waiting for the crib to be empty. But waiting was not idle time. Our imaginations were hard at work devising a workable plan. Waiting for emptiness takes a whole lot of doing.

In early August, the preparations were complete. A chain would be connected to the middle of a sturdy supporting post on the crib. The chain would be anchored to the front-end loader of the Oliver tractor. On Dad's signal, I was to back the tractor up slowly, stopping intermittently until the crib titled at a thirty-degree angle. As the commotion around the corncrib ramped up, Dad walked to several perimeter points, scoping out the best position to take aim at the rats with his gun, given that he was sure the rats would make a chaotic exit.

I eased the tractor into gear and took the slack out of the chain. The crib groaned when it broke free of its cinder block legs as I ever so slowly released the clutch. There was only a two-foot gap between the ground and the crib floor. My eyes were focused on Dad. He started waving his arms high overhead signaling me to stop backing up. As I idled the engine down, the air exploded with loud shooting: POW, POW, POW! Then came sounds of the chamber being cleared of its shells. And then again . . . POW, POW, POW!

This went on for several minutes, and it was then that I saw the mass. The ground appeared to be moving in brown waves that lapped over the high green grass skirting the crib's perimeter. Out of the corner of my eye I saw our neighbor Tom walking hastily toward us, his gun resting on his shoulder. The rats were slowly migrating over to his place, moving into prime real estate. He had money on the table in this deal too. "Didn't think I'd let you have all the fun, did you? Thought you might need some extra fire power," he said to my dad with a grin.

With that, Dad gave the signal for me to inch backward some more. Now the rats were feeling vulnerable and droves of them were making a run for it. They jumped in mighty superhero leaps of faith in all directions at once. Rats the size of innocence to rats the size of holy crap! One tried to climb up the tractor tire, which instantly drew a harrowing scream from the depth of my lungs. POW, POW, POW!

Our dog Spotty was tied up for his own safety. He was barking at a steady pace, but my scream hurled him into a frenzied barking fit. As soon as I was given the okay to abandon the tractor, I did. Dad collected all the rats and buried them. I never knew the final count. The gunfire echoed in my ears for hours.

The corncrib was dismantled and a new, round crib with a solid concrete foundation was erected in the weeks ahead. I don't recall ever seeing another rat on the farm.

Harvests are meant to feed something . . . cattle, ideas, passion, creativity, change. Storing a crop beyond its usefulness robs you of reaping the full benefit of what you've sown. Overabundance invites the weight of stagnation and the cunningness of greasy snake-tailed rodents to infest your corncribs. Life isn't meant to be occupied. It's meant to be lived. There is a limit to our capacity to hold—our capacity to release is limitless.

Fancy Feet

At the threshold of the grain elevator door, the piercing peep of hundreds of baby chicks muddle the conversation taking place between patrons at the desk. Tiny cardboard boxes with rows of one-inch holes popped in all sides are stacked all over the room. Through the holes you can see fuzzy yellow balls mounted atop toothpick legs scampering around their temporary home. Confinement does that. It makes us scared and jittery.

I've left the car running, heater on full blast trying to make the environment cozy for the chicks until we reach home where the heat lamp's hypnotizing glow can put them under the spell of deep sleep. Carefully, I set the excited box down on the seat next to me. They are only one day old and have already endured an incredible journey. It won't be much longer, and they will arrive at their new home made warm and inviting with a bed of clean straw, fresh water, and feed.

Each chick receives a quick once over as I lift them out of the box and set them under the heat lamp's yellow glow. It's not the norm, but all are alive. I am feeling fortunate. The last chick clutched in my fingers is much tinier than the rest, and its toes are curled this way and that. I set this wee one down next to me and watch it for a while. Its deformed toes don't appear to be giving the little chick any problem, just a mere inconvenience to this peep's push to persevere.

Peter, my four-year-old son, has been hovering close since I came home and hasn't stopped talking until now. At this tender age, compassion comes freely and frequently. Lines of concern are being written in the creases on his forehead and his eyes well up with grief. "The little chick will be just fine, Peter," I say in a reassuring voice. "She is going to be more than fine," I reiterate. "God made this little chick special. He gave her fancy feet. Let's name her Fancy!" There— the sadness is falling from his eyes in big drops, and the creases of concern written on his forehead slowly erase.

Fancy got along fine in her life as a Haen hen. Her fancy feet scratched the rich earth of the woods' edge and green fields, alive with things that creep and crawl. Fancy's feet also scratched the surface of our hearts and taught us that if we are lucky enough to share this earth and walk with a relative that has fancy feet, we know what it is to walk in beauty.

Try Acceptance

> "The cow here becomes the symbol of the attitude required to reach the middle. The quiet place in the center of the tension of the opposites, the path to the transcendent function and to the individuation itself. Here we arrive at the type of docility marked by strength and integrity of character and recognition of our own limitations. We find the brightness that illuminates the four quarters of the world."
> —Barbara Hannah, *The Archetypal Symbolism of Animals*

The bovine ensemble, with its marked hides of black-and-white, begins its familiar cacophony of barn noises signaling the onset of evening milking. The cattle chorus wafts through the partially open barn door and floats off beyond the well-traveled, crushed gravel yard up to our white 1950s ranch-style house. My steps lighten and I pick up the beat as I head in the direction of the song.

Neck-chain links clank on iron stanchions as hooves scrape for traction against the smooth resistance of the barn's concrete floor. From a kneeling position, contorted necks and tongues rough as pine bark stretch their reach, sweeping remaining crumbs of their grain portions into wide, bell-shaped feed shovels. They rise from their prayers when I pass through the manger with a broom. The cha-chew-cha-chew beat in the background carries my awareness to the vacuum pump. Creamy white rivers of milk will soon be flowing from the ladies' firm pendulous udders. Dad's cheerful whistle is heard over the clamor, keeping perfect time with the barn song, and my heart does the listening. The tune is funneled into the deep chambers of my heart's inner ear, where the drum of its vibration still resounds.

The lively music of livestock is gradually raising the half-staff spirit of this farm girl in the spring of her teenage years. I've been walking in a tangled thicket of heavy emotions that started a week earlier with the loss of my beloved four-legged heifer named Spunker and her newborn calf. Red eyes puffy from reciting a sustained series of wet prayers have trouble adjusting to the dim lighting of the barn.

Stumbling over the gutter plate as I cross the threshold triggers Spotty into a brief but ferocious barking spasm, announcing my entrance like a bugle call. My nose feels like it's the size of a potato, and a pounding pressure is building behind my sinuses. There comes a time when, as Yoda says, you have to "Try not. Do or do not. There is no try." I'm determined to help Dad with the chores tonight even though he told me I didn't have to. I feel the need to mingle with life again. The tingles of numbness have cauterized the edges of my grieving emotional wounds, and the profuse bleeding of tears is subsiding. I'm coming to know a new kind of acceptance: unconditional acceptance.

All this time later, throwing a pebble of remembrance into those moments ripples emotions in my heart if I dare gaze too long at the reflective pool. "Old Spunker is due next month. You can raise her calf," my dad had said to me. "How about that?" he had added with a hint of joviality. I remember turning away, embarrassed by the excitement his words invoked in me; no doubt I looked like I had just gotten off a two-ticket carnival ride. My back to him, trying to act nonchalant, I had managed to respond with a lackluster shrug.

Today the barn doesn't feel the same without her presence. It's hard to look in the direction of her empty stall, which, a week earlier, I had carefully prepared with a love-thick layer of golden straw. On one of those nights, in the wee hours before the sun kissed the darkness, Dad and

I had impatiently kept vigil over the young Spunker as she labored intensely to deliver her first calf. After many hours of vigilant checks on her progress with nothing to show for her laborious effort, Dad decided it was time we step in and give her a hand.

Drawing on his years of experience, Dad laid out a plan that we both felt was the best one. When my father slipped his arm into the birth canal, it became immediately apparent that the calf was larger than we had first presumed and was stuck. Controlled panic disrupted my normal thinking process and I was relieved to have him start to shout orders at me, which I gratefully followed. "Pull this leg that way when she pushes next time. Roll the other leg away, NOW!" he commanded.

Spunker's mournful moos through the painful contractions rallied us on, together, but we still couldn't make any headway. "Go get the come-along from the shed," Dad directed as he washed his arms and hands of Spunker's bodily fluids. This was a last resort. It meant that Dad, who I believed had the strength to move mountains, did not have enough power on his own to pull this calf out. In dire straits, we had rehearsed this chaotic scene many times before with other first-calf heifers, but when it's your heifer, it's just not the same. There's more at stake; you've been inside the soul of this animal and it's been inside yours. It doesn't matter if you've shared a chapter, a page, or a verse—you are a part of each other's stories, and we all want our "Once upon a times" to have a happy ending.

The heaviness building in each passing minute dragged on our spirits like a rowboat taking on water. Time was at a premium throughout the process, but after Spunker's water broke it was critical that the calf be delivered immediately if it were to have the slightest chance of survival. We pulled together in rhythm with Spunker's contractions, over and over in unison. As soon as I saw the calf's mucus-veiled nose poke through the embryonic sac, I gently swabbed into and around its wet, soft-pink openings, clearing what I could with each swift swipe of my shaking fingers. I deposited the slime across my upper pants leg again and again.

Finally, the head was through! In the next instant, a gush brought the rest of the calf wholly into this world. But there was no gasp for air so we did what we knew to do. We cleared the airway, lifted the head, rubbed the back vigorously with a burlap sack, and blew short puffs of air into its mouth cavity. "Come on! Come on! You can do this! TRY! TRY! BREATHE! BREATHE!"

Words spun in my head, making my sentences dizzy, but the stone-still calf lay flat on its side in the middle of the barn aisle.

The edges of our own existence become frayed when we witness death. In that mysterious moment between living and dying, we recognize that life is fragile.

Dad abruptly turned my attention to Spunker. The lengthy, difficult birth had left her looking tattered and she showed signs of distress from the ordeal. She made no display of interest in the calf, nor any attempt to stand. There was no melody of low moos to reassure the calf.

Taking this in, our focus immediately turned to Spunker's well-being. The urgency was now in getting her to stand on all fours. Any farmer who values the title knows that a down cow will die. Dad tried to rock her, gathering momentum by pushing with his feet next to her hip bones, gaining leverage from the adjoining stall bar, but Spunker remained rigid. I stepped in front of her vulnerability when Dad stomped toward her with the pitchfork and managed to get in a futile jab. Given our efforts, if Spunker had been a beached whale with legs, she would have been standing at that point. There was a want and will, but her back legs just weren't complying and death's gavel was serving her sentence—without a judge or a jury. I had faith that I could overturn the paralyzing verdict if Dad would but give me a chance to try.

Over the next several days I cared for Spunker's every need and provided what comfort I could. Her condition deteriorated but I selfishly refused to give up. One day, when I get home from school, I noticed Uncle Louie's turquoise blue pickup parked tight against the side door of the barn, inside the cow corral. It has a heavy lean toward the back. A vet visit held consequences and, as I sped to the barn, I wasn't sure if my heart or my feet got there first.

I jumped into the back of the pickup with her, adjusting her head to rest on my lap. She will not go to slaughter on my watch! I vow to stand guard against any enemy trying to destroy the fortress our love built. Every part of my being was searching for some other way to save her and I was numb from the long vigil.

Time slipped by that evening without notice . . . dozing emotions drifted me into its hidden passageways . . . a few hours later I surrendered to sleep.

I woke to the distinct sound of Dad rinsing out the milkers. A little later, I heard the scraping noises of him making the final round with the manure shovel, and then the barn was covered in darkness. I could see the glow of a Marlboro dancing along a shadow figure coming toward the truck. When the facial features took form, the shadow speaks: "Come to the house. I'll unload her in the morning."

Dad is a man of principles. He says what he means and means what he says, and I trusted his word completely.

In silence, Dad helps me out of the truck bed and together we walk up to the house with only the sounds of the night making conversation.

The next day was a new day. Like a hungry monarch caterpillar feasting on the edge of a tender milkweed leaf, anticipation had been nibbling at the seconds since I'd stepped on the school bus that morning. All afternoon, I'd been growing fat on the juicy possibilities that second chances could hold.

Once off the bus, I make a mad dash to the barn. There in its nave, hanging from the ceiling, was a menagerie of pulleys and chains attached to an iron bar welded in the shape of a T. Frayed old conveyor belts connected to the aforementioned contraption supported the full weight of Spunker's back end. During the day, Dad had fabricated a "lift" in one of the milking stalls. There, before non-believing eyes, Spunker was standing!

We immediately started a daily physical therapy regimen of gradually putting weight on her legs for short periods of time. Progress, however, eludes us, and after a while, it starts to feel as though "trying" has taken on a life of its own. I had woven "trying" deep Into a skewed core belief, one that ordained that I could never stop trying. Trying became an unassailable "sacred cow," an untouchable belief wherein quitting is never an option, no matter how remote the odds of success.

An opportunity to reassess my meaning of "try" was approaching. The sacred cow was being sacrificed. Could I bring myself to stop trying? I would find out soon enough.

The hide on the sides of Spunker's body looked like a wet towel draped over a washboard, and dullness fogged her looking-glass eyes. The time I spent with her was outside of time; I had little concern where the dials of the barn clock positioned themselves. Change is difficult to see when you deprive yourself of the perspective distance provides. I focused my daily tasks on details pertaining to Spunker's comfort, which conveniently shaded reality with a false glow of rosy-pink progress. I cleaned the manure crusted to her immobile tail and relieved her udder of its small burden of milk. Mostly, though, I'd just talk to her; telling her that I loved her forever.

The lift did something unexpected. It raised the picture that reality was painting and hung it right on my nose. At first, it gave me hope. But the truth was, the eleventh hour had passed and the clock was about to strike twelve. When I woke up to that fact, I asked Spunker if she wanted me to stop trying, for she wasn't improving and she was ready to go. The look of calm acceptance in her eyes told me as much; it spoke to my listening heart. Spunker had peacefully come to a gentle acceptance of her circumstances some while ago and her eyes told me it was my turn to do the same. She was now on the rainbow bridge and I was in her way.

In all this, she was teaching me about gentle acceptance—how to peacefully arrive at an emotional threshold and then how to move through it. With a heavy heart, but knowing it was the right thing to do, I accepted Spunker's reality, and then let her go.

A bitter aftertaste of shame, guilt, self-doubt, and failure welled up inside me. Two painful losses so close together had me gulping down lots of life's big questions. The one I had the most trouble swallowing was accepting what reality is versus what I wanted it to be; I couldn't seem to get that all the way down. Nevertheless, I disassembled my belief system around the notion of "trying." My new unconditional relationship with acceptance meant that the debris left in the aftermath of turbulent experiences no longer built a dam of guilt, shame, or questioning.

Eventually, I found a middle ground between not being afraid to try and not being afraid to stop trying, a place to hold onto if the dam should happen to break.

The intricate melodies of barn songs occasionally strum the taut cords stretched over this scar on my heart. The memory of Spunker and her calf strikes unlikely high notes. I am honored that they taught me to go deeper within myself to better understand the nature of wisdom by honoring what it means to accept what I cannot change. They dismissed the myth that gentleness equals weakness. On the outside I saw Spunker's strength. When she let me see inside, I saw that the source of that strength was a gentle acceptance of life as it is, as it comes, not as we wish it to be.

Two Buckets Full

An empty kindling bucket led to a lesson in mindfulness this morning. It didn't take long to remember how attentive and alert you have to be when your splitting kindling with a hand ax. I never lost awareness of where my fingers were or the steadiness of the piece of wood that the ax was about to come down on. After filling two kindling buckets, I was darn near a Buddhist monk!

It only takes a few minutes of mindful motion to feel an energetic recharge. Not only does it balance the mind and body but it can make you more aware of when you are becoming imbalanced.

An empty life can fill with meaning as painlessly as two kindling buckets with a mindful practice. Maybe it's time to ask yourself, like the title of the wonderful children's book, "Have you filled your bucket today?"*

* *Have You Filled Your Bucket Today? For Kids* was written by Tom Rath and Mary Reckmeyer (2009).

Any "Birdie" Home?

The hum of my early morning barn chores is temporarily paused to listen to the prayerful song of returning migratory birds. With each passing day, a growing variety has been calling our home theirs. From the woods, I hear the unmistakable throaty flute-like song of the wood thrush. Not to be out-sung, an Eastern phoebe, perched on its favorite maple tree, joins in with a two-part song that it is named for: "fee-bee, fee-bee." The phoebe family has been returning to the mud and grass nest they constructed under our eave for the past ten or so years. It's the warbling, musical whistle coming from the direction of our prairie that turns my ear away from all the other melodies. The expressive song is soft and gentle. As I make my way to a good viewing position of the nest box mounted in the prairie, I see a glint of azure blue flicker on the ground. The most heavenly blue I know. *Zip-a-Dee-Doo-Dah*, the bluebirds are back!

In the mid-twentieth century, the Eastern bluebird numbers plummeted, mostly due to the depletion of nesting habitat—rotted out fence-line posts. Due to the efforts of many organizations and nature-loving people, the bluebird population has rebounded. Gardeners are richly repaid for attracting bluebirds to their yards as their diet consists almost entirely of insects. Long before backyard gardeners, farmers cultivated this beneficial friendship. In the beginning of the conservation work, farmers led the way by creating "bluebird trails" on their land. Open fields near wooded areas are a favorite habitat. People once understood the importance of these interspecies relationships. Unfortunately, it seems to be something we have to relearn. My experience with the bluebirds gives me hope.

Thanks to an environmentally conscious uncle and his gift of a bluebird nest box, I became part of the efforts to bring their population back from the brink of extinction in the 1980s. We banded fledglings, counted pairs, and kept records on brood batches. I am eternally grateful for my early introduction to "blue birding." I still have the gifted nest box. It's nearly thirty years old and usually one of the first nest boxes of the dozen or more around our property to be claimed by a mated pair.

The delightful gentle greeting of the bluebird's song each spring reminds me of the worthiness in friendships—relationships forged and fortified over time; together, each one saves the other. We must be vigilant of the fragile friendships we have with the natural world. I believe in the undeniable strength of our interrelatedness. It's much better to think of ourselves as a part of the whole than a piece apart. After all, we are all living life together.

Note: It's always a good idea to attach entrance predator guards to help limit predation of the nest box. Sassy kitties can put their paws in but they can't reach down and get at the young birds. Remember to clean out the box after each brood has fledged. The bluebirds will build a new nest on top of the old nest material with each hatching (one to four each season), raising the nest dangerously close to the entrance hole.

Whistle on a Whim

In memory of Edward Galkowski Sr.

You don't hear much whistling anymore. Dad whistled his song of life, a gift that unbeknown to him brought happiness to many over his lifetime. There is playfulness to a sound made through puckered lips, the air tongue-tickled as the breath's bellows pump, making music on the inhale and exhale, the breath of life's soul music.

His favorite tune was merry and light, the chorus at the forefront of my memory. I don't think a day went by that I didn't hear that tune when I worked alongside him. He loved to whistle during milking time on our dairy farm. The melody danced between the clang of cow chains against iron stalls and through the persistent chug of the vacuum pump. The sound relaxed and eased the cattle. When we worked outside the sound of his whistle was clear and free, traveling far to spread the cheer of his spirit. For some reason even the faint sound of his whistle drew attention. It had a way of calling you home—calling your heart. At Dad's funeral, I became aware of the distance his whistle traveled into the hearts of our neighbors, far and near, and how missed it was going to be.

I have memory moments when I expect to hear his whistle. As if I could will it to travel through the dimensions of space and time. My ear searching for the sound only my heart can now hear. Every now-and-again, usually when I'm working on a problem alone, I start to whistle Dad's song, and I am called home. I'm called to listen to my heart, and the answer comes.

Dad passed in spring when the spirit of a new season is ushered in with the songbird's whistle and the nightly chorus of peepers, those tiny frogs with the loud chirp, echoing over fields of hope and promise. He left at a time when everything held a song in their heart. Dad had a simple pure-noted purpose in his lifetime. He was a fixer; he worked at fixing life—for his family, friends and neighbors, the earth, his animals and crops. His life was alive with the sound of his own music. What a gift to give yourself. Whistling kept him in tune with his heart, his life a living song.

I can whistle, not as well as Dad, but it's not stopping me from living to the beat of my own heart like Dad, and occasionally, I put my lips together and blow.

Folded Hands

The one physical feature about my Dad that I remember the most, second to his sky-blue eyes, was his hands. His fingers were cucumber-like, thick skinned and rectangular from a lifetime of physical outdoor work. The skin, a tanned leather color and tough as a pig's nose. as a child, I don't ever remember a time when they weren't stained with grease or covered with cuts and scrapes.

I recall one winter Dad almost cut his thumb clear off where it attached to his hand with a chainsaw. I watched as he came to the kitchen sink, calmly unwrapped the red hanky twisted around his fingers and asked me to get a towel. The sink ran red as the water washed over the wound. The skin at the base of his thumb was jagged and shredded where the chainsaw caught it. He never let out a cry of pain. Only a few choice cuss words. He was giving me orders to gather what he needed—peroxide, gauze, duct tape—and to run to the barn and get the iodine bottle next to the vacuum pump. Amazingly, he had full movement. The bone wasn't cut, so in time the wound healed but it drained and oozed something terrible for the longest time.

After barn chores, Dad would sit on the chair in the basement where he took off his barn boots and gently unwrap the gauze around the wound. Then he would call over our dog Spotty to lick the wound. When Spotty had thoroughly tongue-washed the thumb, Dad dumped peroxide on, leaving the wound open to dry. He never was much for bandages. The thumb healed perfectly.

If you happened to pass him driving in the pick-up, you could count on getting a wave. Well, it wasn't exactly a wave, it was the lifting of his right index finger off the steering wheel, sticking straight in the air like a pole while the other fingers remained gripped to the wheel. A few folks actually shared this memory with me—Ed's wave they called it.

Any time Dad picked up a shovel, fork, or hoe he spit in his hands to get a better grip. I carry on the tradition to keep a good grip on Dad's memory.

Of all my hand memories of Dad, the most poignant one was seeing them folded in prayer with his head cradled deep inside his palms as he knelt at the side of his bed in prayer. Every night you could hear him mumbling his words to God into those thick cucumber fingers. Every night.

Hay Day

It has been an unusually soggy summer here in northeast Wisconsin—both in rain and humidity. Instead of making second or thirds crops this time of year, most farmers are just getting off their first crop. The worry that comes with the struggle to harvest hay is getting real. That was until a four-day break in the weather was forecast two weeks ago. How quickly lack can turn into abundance if we are willing to seize the opportunity, even if it means a whole lot of hard work. The inspiration for this piece.

Bronze skin leather tough
Drenched in salty drops
Thirst burns
I drink in the sky
Prayers pour out of my heart
Machinery and God be merciful
Long windrows lay ready to make perfect hay
Keep breakdowns and tears of dark clouds away
Bound tight with twine square bales bulge
Full wagons waddle over the bald field
Each one—together—enough
Winter's hunger aches for your green
As stars usher in night's moist breath
I walk up to the house feeling spiritually quenched
Exhausted muscles and mind rest peacefully in gratitude's joy
Hard work fears me

part three

Smile Pile

Tickle My Heart

*"A smile's sweet fragrance tickles the heart's soft places.
You feel the giggle."*
—Angie Haen

This section was inspired by little moments of joy that brought a smile to my face as I went about my day. I journaled the joy for quite some time and now I share the delight it gave me then and now with you. I hope they tickle your heart and you feel the giggle.

Things that made me smile today:

The little boy that came on the bus announcing he was going to be good today. "You're good every day," I respond dishonestly. He looks right at me and responds honestly, "No, I'm not."

The black cat that waits at the end of the driveway with the kids for the school bus. The cat waits, sitting like a statue by their feet until I pull away. Then the creature nonchalantly gets up, turns toward the house, and walks up the drive. Such a display of loyalty and bravery in this cold!

The little girl on my shuttle that came up to chat about the extreme cold weather. She told me that her dad told her it was twenty below zero with the windshield, and there was no telling her the correct word was windchill because her DAD told her it was windshield!

People leaving their shopping carts in the parking lot at Super Ron's. I'm assuming the extreme cold was the cause of the departure from the politeness of returning the carts to the return area. Half the parking lot was strewn with strays. I took it upon myself to corral the ones near my car. As I was walking back to gather a few more, I was pleasantly surprised to see I had help. Several other patrons had "bombed" my random act of kindness. Magic happens when you wheel the wand of kindness.

Seeing twinkling Christmas lights on the houses along my bus route in the morning and afternoon routes as my hunger for light grows. They are a good distraction from winter's grumbling belly.

All my four-year-olds who ride to school dressed in snow boots, snow pants, winter jackets, hats, and gloves. That means I can't even think about turning on the heat or we spend twenty minutes at school, trying to figure out what goes to whom. Tomorrow I will dress like a four-year-old.

Dandelion bouquets I receive each spring from one or more of my student riders. This morning I received my first of the season. Over the years I've noticed that when little boys give me bouquets, the flower heads are always moshed and mashed.

My old gardening friend, a rather large garter snake. He has returned to our yard to feast on creepy crawlies in my flower beds. No matter how vigilant I am as I putz in the gardens, I am guaranteed several encounters that will make me gasp for air and clutch my heart with my hand.

The wee four-year-old boy who walked to the van on this rainy morning dressed in rubber from head to toe; rubber rain jacket, rubber boots, rubber hat. AND just to make sure not a single raindrop touched him, he carried an umbrella!

Watching my kitty Misty trying to catch the plops of raindrops as they splashed down on the driveway.

Having a few moments to stand under the horse shelter to listen to the rain ping off the tin roof with the sound of horses chewing hay in the background. The thought about how these raindrops could turn to snowflakes any second made me savor the sound. Snow shushes the landscape. It doesn't ping or sing. Happy I was able to smile through the rain today.

The gentleman I saw walking up a long driveway to retrieve the mail on this below zero day. When the bus cleared the snowbank, I saw he was wearing a furry Elmer Fudd hat, heavily insulated snowmobile boots, a t-shirt and short, SHORT, shorts!

All the 4-k kiddos wound up tight from the Valentine's Day activities. I asked one little boy if he got his girlfriend a valentine. He paused, raised two chubby fingers in front of my face, then proudly stated, "I have two."

The eagle I saw soaring in a circle on my route.

A four-year-old on my van asking me a question. She started out accidentally with Mama instead of Ms. Angie.

Wally walking behind me on the packed path made by my snowshoes. It was getting late, and I guess he was tired. I started to trip-up every so often. Something was wrong. I stopped to check my straps. As I swiveled to look behind me, I found the problem. Wally was standing squarely on the back of both my snowshoes. He had been following so closely he was stepping on the backs of my snowshoes. Apparently, I wasn't keeping up to the speed of the smells.

A little girl singing—and other things—in the bathroom. I needed to use the bathroom at ABVM (Assumption of the Blessed Virgin Mary) school during my ten minute layover between routes. The little girl in the stall next to me was singing a hymn. There was a pause in the singing. The silence was momentarily interrupted by a distinct kerplunk sound. Singing continued and ended with a nice round of alleluias.

The mouse that I thought was dead in Wally's food bag but turned out to be very much alive. A healthy scream and Wally and Andy come running to my rescue—in that order. Andy got the cat. I tipped the bag over and the very full mouse scampered, no, walked, barely moving to a safe place. The cat sat with her butt firmly pressed on the ground. Tail twitching. Watching in amusement.

Finally organizing a writing area. Joy! Joy! Joy!

Having Sophie join me in yoga classes at the Abrams Community Center. There's only so many things a seventeen-year-old wants to do with Mom—especially since I don't shop or do my nails.

A kindergartner on my bus politely asking me if wearing pajamas was allowed on the bus. I replied, "If it's pajama day. It's tomorrow, huh?" A nod yes was his reply followed by, "You can wear yours too!"

Peter getting up at 4:30 am to turkey hunt before school then sending me the picture of the sunrise. It made me feel like we did a few things right along the way.

The little girl on my shuttle route who asked me for a plastic bag to put her gym clothes in because she believed her cat peed on them—a habit the cat got into when school started. As I turned to give her the plastic bag, she promptly shoved the urine-soaked clothes in my face. "Do you smell it?" she asked. All I can say is that she wasn't lying.

The ladies at the hair salon that went all goo-goo over my gray hair. Not kidding! Gray hair is apparently "in." Well, I'll have gray hair when it's "out" too.

Getting a text from my eighty-year-old mother-in-law from her shiny new iPhone.

Wet Wally shoving his nose, then the rest of his big old self, between my legs in an effort to dry off. Not sure how dry he got, but he did deposit a good amount of water and wet yellow fur on my inner thighs. He seemed delighted that I now shared his discomfort. Misery loves company.

Observing Creator's propensity to be creative with the weather as of late.

My last student off, a second grader, who is usually sleeping. If I don't see his head leaning over the side of the seat, I ask him over the PA to "show me the hand," and up from behind a seat pops a hand raised high in the air, signaling he IS awake. Tonight, he was at the edge of the front seat. "Not sleepy this afternoon?" I asked. He responds, "Ms. Angie, I have to go pee really bad. I've been holding it the whole ride." Fortunately, he lives in a wooded area. Without giving it a second thought, I say to him, "Maybe you better scoot behind one of those trees if you can't make it to the house." Which he did. Then I had the second thought. If there's a little note on my keys tomorrow that says, "Angie, please stop in the office," I'll know why.

It's good to know a few Pulaski High School football players. It gives you depth in the hay baling position when your first string is in Crandon watching off-road racing. For the third and final time this summer, I laid down hay.

Erik Knutzen wrote in a post from February 23, 2015: "A beehive is a living thing, not a machine for our exploitation. I'm a natural beekeeper and feel that honey harvests must be done with caution and respect. To us, beekeeping is, at the risk of sounding a little melodramatic, a sacred vocation. We are in relationship with our backyard hive and feel our role is to support them and to very occasionally accept the gift of excess honey. What we get we consider precious and use for medicine more than sweetening."

It's been a honey of a day! In gratitude to Creator's tiny helpers for manifesting sweet abundance. As a "thank you," we planted one last plot of buckwheat.

Happened upon a movie last night with my all-time favorite actor, Robert Duvall. *Secondhand Lion*. Good clean movie with many hidden meanings. I loved this quote by Duvall's character Hub: "Sometimes the things that may or may not be true are the things a man needs to believe in the most. That people are basically good; that honor, courage, and virtue mean everything; that power and money, money and power mean nothing; that good always triumphs over evil; and I want you to remember this, that love—true love—never dies. You remember that, boy. You remember that. Doesn't matter if it's true or not. You see, a man should believe in those things because those are the things worth believing in."

The flock of cedar waxwings that cleared every berry from our crabapple tree and other fruit-bearing shrubbery throughout our yard. That's exactly why I planted them ten years ago.

Driving Mr. Wally around the estate this morning in the Country Cadillac—our thirty-five-year-old Suzuki four-wheeler. He's getting old and enjoys the leisurely ride around the territory he used to run. When we reach the "hot spot" across the road, he jumps out. Too much to smell! Then I can't get him in! Mr. Wally loves his morning rides. It's becoming a daily routine. I'm alright with being his chauffeur because of the good conversation and company we keep.

I drove the high school boys football team to a game at Bay Port last night. I went into the school to use bathroom. A few stalls down I could hear a mom and her little girl. The mom wanted her to hurry up and get her business done but the little girl was singing one of those sweet made-up songs that musically goes all over the place and just doesn't seem to have a good place to end. I preferred her singing to mom's complaining.

Pulaski won in the final seconds by two points. Lungs got cleaned out from screaming. Late in the evening when I dropped the team at the high school, the coach instructed one player to "pick the garbage off the floor, make sure the windows are shut and nothing is left on the bus. I want the floor CLEAN." The kid was practically on his hands and knees. I thanked him as he was leaving and asked how he got picked for that job. With a smile he said," I'm the team captain. The captain always cleans the bus. Coach doesn't want being the captain to go to my head." Well done, Coach. A lesson in humility he will always remember. Bravo!

"Sometimes your joy is the source of your smile, but sometimes your smile can be the source of your joy."
—Thich Nhat Hanh

part four

Places to Pause

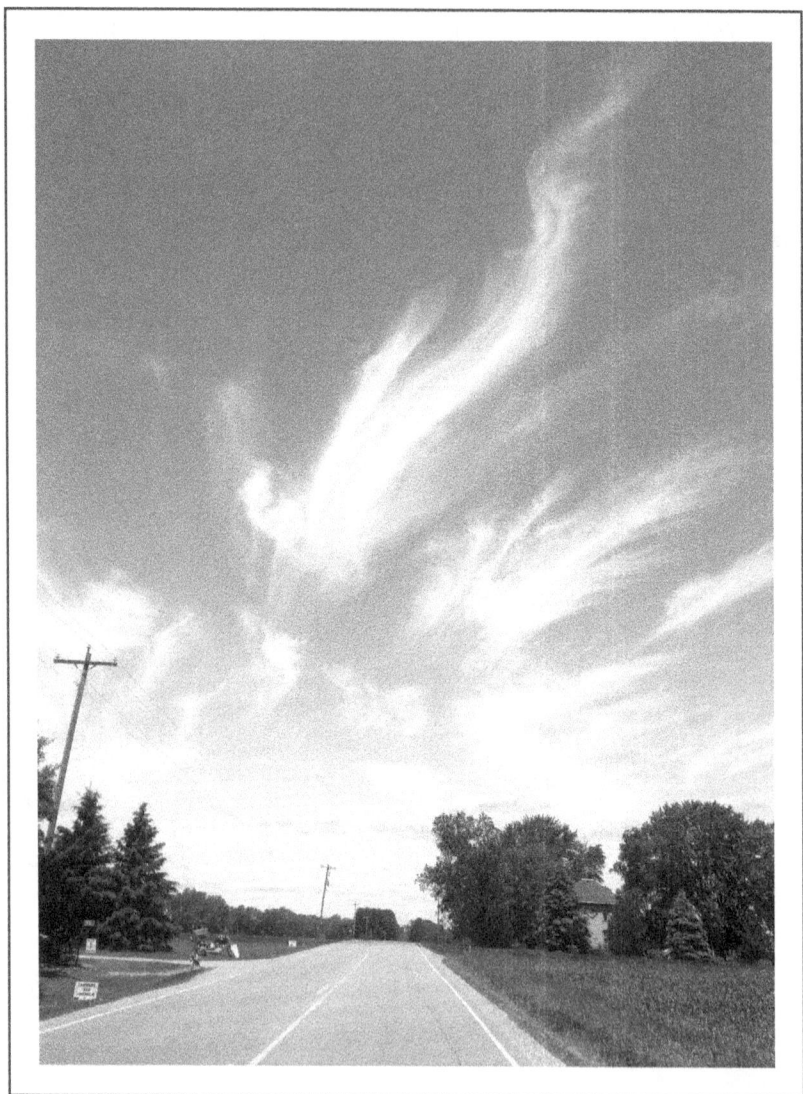

Birth of Beginnings

Winter's seeds are sown.
Beneath me I feel the pregnant earth.
She is swollen; soft and opening.
Preparing for what comes next.
Aliveness passes through vulnerability.
Haven't we all felt that push?
Been in that tight place?
Forced to bring change into the world.
I watched suffering bear down on the skinny fox
and wounded deer.
One fed the other and for both, the anguish ended.
That knowing gave me solace.
Within the circle of life,
the womb of creation is held.
Light comes sooner and stays longer these days.
It burns through Winter's heavy cloak of cold;
vanishing with it, misery and madness.
Oh, to see the land kissed by green again!
To hold all its babies, close to my heart!
Restless with anticipation,
giddy with excitement,
I wait for Spring to take its first breath;
the birth of beginnings.

Let Go of the Rain

In the circle of seasons, fall is a restless spirit. These deep months of autumn are one last raucous hurrah before the weather turns the somber corner toward winter's reverent quiet. Radiant wild leaves mere moments earlier burned the sky's blue, float like embers from a forest aflame. The confetti-colored earth is a sign that winter's wait is ending. Summer's party is over.

Chilly north winds usher in a steady stream of gray clouds heavy with rain. For days the dampness soaks deep down into the bones of the land. An earthy scent lingers in the air like the perfumed smoke of incense. There is nothing like that smell to freshen one's state of mind. All it washes over is cleansed and purified for the coming journey inward to connect with self.

Seasonal transitions can be unsettling. They are raw elemental movement measurable in the mindfulness I keep on my mood. Nature is forcing us to face our feelings. In my way of thinking, her influence on our mind isn't to bring our spirits down as much as it is for us to find ways to raise them up.

Each fall is unique. This year the rain has been persistent and significant. For the most part I've been able to keep a sunny disposition despite the seemingly endless string of gloomy gray days. Making monstrous kettles of homemade soup is a delicious way to shine a soul or two . . . or ten.

This fall taught me that when you can't hold the heaviness of dark clouds any longer let go of the rain.

Come Again

It's coming
Ushered in on Spring's promise
humanities' aesthetic rebirth is coming.
I hear the pant of deliverance.
Almost there
Anticipation's innocence
carries a soul
through heavy fear
and thick uncertainty.
Pushes us through deep blackness.
It's time
The rite of passage has arrived.
Tolerances fully dilated.
Anxiously waiting to hear the wail
from our infant humanness.
All the world rejoices!
It's here
Wrapped in the World's love
Compassion forgives the sin
Reach out your arms
Come
Visit the prayer you prayed.
Hold joy.
Love and be loved.
We journey toward no end.
It's coming—again.

Spruce Up

Good thing my cape wasn't at the laundromat. Our kitty Misty got herself in a predicament. She's been a lover of heights since she was a kitten, spending long moments in the arms of a favored oak tree growing in our yard. But on this day, her adventurous side left her stranded fifty feet above the ground in a blue spruce tree.

At first, I ignored her panicked howls, thinking she got herself into this mess, she can get herself out. Cats are natural aerialists. The calls continued as I finished my chores. Wally spotted her first and began incessantly barking as he made tiny hops up from a sitting position. Nose pointed like a rigid index finger to her position. Misty had moved as far out on the branch as she could to attract my attention, meowing piteously. The louder she meowed the harder Wally bounced. I moved around the large spruce in a wide arc until I found a gap large enough for my body to fit between the picky and sticky boughs.

Coaxing a frightened kitty to the tree's trunk was accomplished with little more than verbal encouragement and wiggly fingers. It was the down part that Misty found complicated. She had to figure out how to descend while still facing up, so the curve of her claws could hold her up; not letting her fall. After an hour, she was able to shimmy down to a manageable jumping distance and took a leap of faith. Not the best landing form but she was no worse for wear, and I came out of it smelling like a spruce. The next time Misty wants to reach new heights, I hope she's learned the best way to navigate obstacles is to keep your chin up and everything will fall into place.

"Believe you can and you're half way there."
—Theodore Roosevelt

Deep Softness

All winter under a white shawl of snow and cold, Mother Earth's dreams kept her buried in warmth below the frost line. The line is gradually melting away and I feel her stir beneath my feet, her deep softness rising. All of Mother Earth's children are opening. Our brothers and sisters living in nature remember the gift of opening is to let light and warmth out as much, maybe even more, as it is to let it in. Spring, the season for our deep softness to rise and shine.

Spring Heraldry

On this, the calendar's last day of winter,
my glance is drawn toward the bouncing
crab apple branches to my right.

They're laden with a feast of red wrinkled
berries for a winged-one. I saw the round
bird's gray-brown feathers with warm
orange underparts flutter joyfully by.
On wings of anticipation the migration
prayer has been consummated.
Spring's ambassador has returned!
The vernal song hibernating within us is
aroused.

"Cheerily, cheer up, cheer up, cheerily, cheer up"!

The Robin sings.
On this, the calendar's first day of spring.

Heart of Pine

As a child I would steal away time from my farm chores to play among the white pines that grew wide and tall next to our land. They grew best in the course, sandy, well-drained soils on the top of small hills. On windy days the sway of the boughs motioned to me like the repeated curl of an index finger beckoning closer. This time of play among the peaceful pines strengthened my spirit's gentleness.

Nothing escapes pine's restful rapture. In their company the spirit wanders free and easy. Whose soul isn't soothed by the faintest tinge of pine's tranquil scent? Gazing at the whorl of branches rise and fall, my consciousness slides effortlessly into the flow of contentment. In the gentle whisper of the pine, I hear wonder's wisdom.

Many people wish for a heart of oak, but I long for a heart of peaceful pine.

Bee Joy

The cleanup crew has arrived! Easy access to a food source doesn't go unnoticed for long by the honeybee. After the honey extraction is complete, all the equipment and empty honey supers are set out for the bees. I took delight in watching them collect every last hint of honey. I could hear and feel their joy vibrating through the air. Maybe they even felt some relief, knowing they won't have to "make" all the honey that will sustain them through the cold dark days ahead.

As I sat mesmerized by ceremonial procession from frames to hive, it occurred to me that I was feeding on the bee's joy. We have easy access to joy's existence. It's all around and in everything. Joy's sweetness increases each time it's shared. We need only allow the joy of others, imagined or real, to be ours.

Like Grass

I want to be like grass after a long white winter and grow green as soon as a thaw wakes my roots.

I want to be like grass in bright blue spring and be reborn.

I want to be like grass in hot red summer and grow no matter how close to the ground people cut me.

I want to be like grass in the crisp brown fall and grow down deep so my roots can anchor me through long white winters, bright blue springs, and hot red summers.

Holy Hive

Reluctantly, I turn up the edge of my wool hat, exposing an ear's tender thin skin to the air's frosty bite. I feel the white flesh turning pink then bright red as the sharp prickle travels down deeper and further into the ear tissue. I momentarily suspend my breathing as I firmly press the naked ear to the hive wall. Sealing out all the noise I can, hoping to funnel in the familiar soothing hum of the hive, hinting that winter's wickedness hasn't desecrated the hives holiness.

Early on in our beekeeping venture, these late-winter checks filled me with strong worry. Six years and four hives later, my faith and trust in our ability to keep bees alive over winter has grown, but with the abundance of evil's rising against the bee, I still rely heavily on God's ear hearing the hum of my prayers.

One of the biggest contributors to a hive's winter survival is having ample food stores. Bees create a substance in the hive known as beebread. The secret recipe is a mixture of honey, pollen, and bee saliva. A process of fermentation breaks down the pollen's protein, which is indigestible in its natural state. Beebread is an invaluable high-energy food source.

Beebread is also known as "food of the Gods." How appropriate! A bee's life work is creating a space to unite the gift of light with the gift of darkness. They are Creator's original light workers! Bees show us that when we bring our Spirit's light into our soul's darkness, we can make a honey of a life.

May you receive honey's sweet sacrament. Take communion from the buds and blooms of Creator's Divinity.

Blessed be thy bee. Holy is thy hive.

Old Life

They came before the sunbeams pierced the darkness. Two sets of heart-shaped foot prints lead to, travel around, and then away from the small hills of corn I placed at the woodland's edge, an offering to the wild things to gather strength and sustenance during an extended period of sub-zero temperatures. No remnants of the corn's golden shell remain. To see my small hills of goodwill consumed fills my heart with joy.

From the size of the tracks, I decide it's a doe and her offspring from last year. Others have come too: a rabbit, a field mouse, and several crows, but it's the deer tracks that take hold of my imagination. It's safe for me to assume the doe is eating for two or three. The burden of nourishing the new life in her womb and her own life is greatest at this time of year. The shrubs and forages they have been eating over the long winter are depleted and spring growth hasn't begun. It's truly a time of life or death for some in the herd.

Soon her instincts will cause her to drive off the yearling. She does this to focus all her energy on raising this year's vulnerable fawn(s). The yearling's old life will come to an abrupt end. I'll probably see it wandering around the fields looking lost and confused for a few weeks. Independence will come at a high price for some; crossing roads safely is a skill taught by experience. Others will adapt well to this time of transition, venturing out into a new way of living without hesitation, being an example of gentle strength and resilience for all of us.

The thoughts of the big changes ahead for the yearling stayed with me as I walked on. The enduring trust the doe placed in her instincts is indomitable. She has clear knowledge that it is a lesson she can't teach her yearling.

Trusting its instincts is something the yearling can only learn by being driven off to live a new way. Nature reminds me of life's continual cycle of renewal. Harsh as that may be at times, life never gets old. As the years pass, I am beginning to understand that life doesn't grow old. I do.

Stuff and Fluff

Soon nature will outfit my horses—Chief Lakota, Duchess, and Jazz—with heavy, thick winter coats. During the winter I affectionately nickname them Fluffy, Puffy, and Stuffy—respectfully, of course. Jazz, my mini-Appaloosa, could actually keep his winter nickname all year long. It describes his soft, round physique perfectly! The biggest reason I overlook his aptitude to find mischief is his charming resemblance to a child's plush stuffed animal. Jazz is stuffed with cuteness!

The change in my horses' coats is slight at first. It comes one hair at a time, thickening and rising as daylight hours dwindle and the mercury slides further down the thermometer. Slow, gentle change from the inside out is a gift we, whether human being or animal, give ourselves.

Winter's thick, heavy thoughts are right around the corner too. Like trapped air between hair strands, we insulate ourselves from cold, bitter experiences, their shiver inescapable in the wintry season of introspection. The winter of the mind exposes raw hurt feelings. Their pain can no longer be protected under a blanket of fear. Self-reflection bares our souls; the naked soul is truth's mirror.

Come spring, the harshness of winter sheds. If we are willing to see ourselves clearly—work through all the stuff and fluff—we will enter the soul's summer sleek and shiny. When we open the hurt, the wounds close.

Horseback Haiku

Gust of fretfulness
Hooves fly to freedom's escape
Stay between the ears!

Choked Oak

For a very long time, the sight of this oak tree draped sadness over my heart. Later, anger for the person(s) that long ago forgot the heavy chain wrapped around its trunk. The tree was a solid anchor for the chain length stretched across the driveway keeping unwelcome trespassers from easy access to the fertile hunting land. Nailed midway up into the tree's trunk, a sign hung with the words "KEEP OUT." The unforgiving rusty chain had tightened around the majestic oak's trunk. So merciless was its chokehold that the chain, barely visible in some areas, had become embedded in the bark. I imagined a slow painful torture, the chain and tree no longer separated from each other. How like life, I thought. We all have things we can't free ourselves from, but they don't have to keep us from growing.

I knew the reality of the situation. No longer could the oak tree free itself from the embedded chain. Doing so would kill the tree. The bark is what transports the water and nutrients through the tree. If the circumference of the tree trunk is bare of its bark, the tree dies, unable to transport nutrients and pass water through the wounded area.

If a tree encounters something in its way, the tree has two choices: grow away or grow around. There may be a slowing but there is no stopping a growing tree. The choked oak is a testament to that. In time, the oak will entirely consume the chain, a graceful melding of acceptance over restriction. Hidden beneath the bark, the oak's unseen wound will give no indication that there was ever anything that tried to stop it from reaching its full potential.

People put their own mental and emotional chains across the paths to their unlimited potential, anchored deep in the unforgiving restrictions of a closed mind or closed heart. Simply choose a direction to grow and you will create an opening for the mind and heart to expand. Don't let a chain of regret choke your dreams.

Small Feelings

Leisure activities elude me for the most part, unless I consciously fold them into my daily routine, as I did this morning. I began seeing butterflies everywhere while moving the horse's pasture fence, and soon I couldn't resist the invitation they offered to come and flutter around with them among the milkweed, black-eyed Susans and coneflowers. Butterflies are the embodiment of graceful transformation and beauty. Butterflies open an awareness and energy of another way of being. They seem to float on invisible waves. Instead of catching butterflies, I caught my mind fluttering. Delighted with the pause to ponder they inspired. It's good to feel small sometimes.

Ever Green

Crumbling colorless leaves blanket the ground in a thick layer, giving our woodsy path a spongy surface for my boots to land. Wet from the steady cold rain, some leaves cling to my soles like a frightened child's arms locked around its mother's neck. Familiar shapes of maple, oak and poplar now unrecognizable; a few weeks ago their flaming colors burnt up the sky's blue. Then November's wind of change came blowing the fire out of the trees, spreading it onto the ground. The brilliant sparks in hues of orange, red, and yellow exploding into the air, landing on the forest floor like confetti, signaling the end of fall's magical celebration of transition.

Distorted by the elements, our woodsy trail is now littered with the colorless season of death and dying. I love the earthy smell during this time of transition. It focuses my senses on the renewal and not the rot. Transitions can make us feel like that—colorless, empty. It's in these moments that I look toward the evergreens, white pine especially, my favorite variety.

Seeing their burst of green on late autumn's dull brown landscape always brightens my spirits. When winter's white blanket is drawn up close over the sleeping countryside, those scattered patches of green give me strength to endure and hope for the future. Evergreens face the fierce north wind and heavy snow burden of Wisconsin's winter storms without complaint. If only we could offer forgiveness so easily to our burdens and have faith in our spiritual roots to hold strong against all those things that make us squint.

Two lungs full of a pine's clean fresh scent washes the dead right out of winter. I admire the evergreen family and its unique ability to grow green through all the seasons. How splendid it must be to pass through all of life's seasons feeling ever green.

part five

Give and Thank

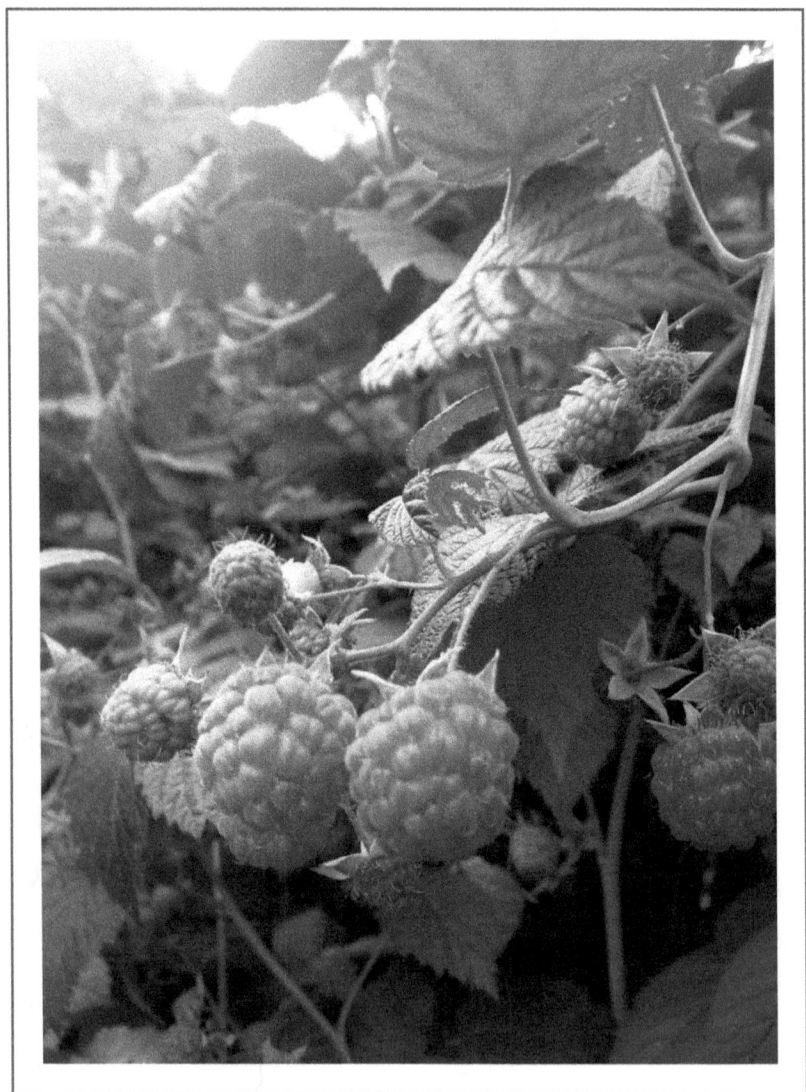

Give and Thank

I am grateful for you!Expressions of gratitude tap into a deep-down internal force that instantaneously shifts negative energy into positive power. Having a daily gratitude practice is a wonderful way to find a positive path on any journey you are on. As they say: Practice doesn't make perfect, it makes progress.

Make every day a happy day of giving thanks!

Pick'n and a Grin'n

Fall, the peak of harvest time, tugs at my good farm roots. The air takes on a sweet earthy smell. In every direction, the land's bountiful gifts lay over the fields like a table set for a feast.

When farmsteads were first established, it was customary to have an apple orchard, usually planted close to house and heart. Planting an apple orchard was a priority when our home was built. The scent of apple blossoms perfuming the air in late spring is like the breath of an angel. The aroma of apple anything emanating from an oven enhances the spirit of the dreariest soul. A crop of apples gives me a plentiful harvest of happiness.

"The pickles aren't gonna pick themselves. The cows aren't gonna milk themselves." This was one of my mom's favorite directives when I was growing up. There seemed to be an infinite number of things that couldn't get done by themselves. During autumn's bounty on our small dairy farm, harvest season had no end. The difficulty can be in discerning when enough is enough. There is no greater feeling of contentment that I know of than having enough— enough hay to make it through the winter; enough preserves in the pantry; enough time; enough love. More times than not, enough meant rolling up your shirt sleeves and wiping sweat from your brow. Fall, in the peak of its bountiful harvest is a time when I feel the essence of what enough is; it's the feeling of thankfulness that fills you with contentment.

Our apple trees are bearing fruit. The crop is good but not as good as in years past. I was raised to believe that happiness in one's life requires a certain amount of effort. You have to work at being happy. Gathering happiness may necessitate going out on a limb, but it's there hanging on every branch on the tree of life. Happy doesn't always come to you. You have to go out and get happy.

As I gather up the deliciousness of the apple harvest, I come to understand a wider perspective on things that can't get done by themselves—like being happy. Happiness doesn't fill you unless you are grateful, and feeling grateful is about not letting it matter whether you have a handful of apples in your bushel basket or you have enough to fill it up. It's in the doing that happiness is harvested. The fullness of gratitude makes the smallest happiness fill you with enough.

Apples to Apples

Summer is drowsy, ready for sleep.
A dreamy scent perfumes the breeze.
Youth's green tang mellows.
Tart and hard: surrender
to sweet pink and easy yellow.
Wolf River. Prairie Spy. Lodi. Zestar.

Voluptuous ornaments adorn
each limb's length.
Rosy streaks from stem to blossom end
graceful as swan necks, the branches bow.
Fruit at perfection's peak now!
McIntosh. Cortland. Red Delicious. Granny Smith.

Teeth crush down through tender flesh.
Taste the ripeness
in a season's end.
Juices run apple-soul deep, blue-sky wide.
Wipe your chin ready
from side to side.
Gala. Sweet Tango. Empire. Golden Crisp.

Spirit Food

I woke early on a Sunday when the phone rang at 7:15 am.
It was Marie, my brother-in-law's elderly mother. She was
unable to attend a gathering at our home the day before,
so I sent a container of apple French toast along with Re-
nee and Tom for her to enjoy later. Marie is rich in years—
eighty-five, I believe. She is fiercely independent and casts
a wide net when it comes to things that interest her, which
provides plenty of fodder for us to chew on during our conversations.

She called to express her genuine gratitude for the
dish that provided her with not one but two meals and her
amazement that I can cut apples so thinly by hand. We took
the opportunity to chat a bit. Food nourishes the spirit as
well as the body, as I let the delicious feeling of appreciation
Marie served up fill my soul.

Happy day of giving thanks!
Fill everyday with gratitude.
Feast on the good.
Feel the fullness of a good life lived well.

Harvest Happy

Most days now begin before the warmth of the sun has had a chance to drink up the dew clinging to smooth blades of grass. Nonetheless, I've taken precautionary measures. I know the sun will be high and mighty before I'm through harvesting the garden's bounty. Stretched across my brow, a bandanna folded over itself several times to secure hair and soak up sweat. We're at the tail end of the dog days of summer here in Wisconsin, but the sultry weather is hanging around like a bad case of fleas.

Basket in hand, I head to the peace of the berry patch to harvest abundance. The thing about abundance of any kind is seeing it through to the harvest. However you bring abundance into your life—growing it, attracting it, or visualizing it—know that you will have to pick it, preserve it, and participate in distributing it. Prosperity is all around us, rotting on the vine.

If there is one universal law everyone forgets, it's the Law of Action. To manifest anything in our lives, we need to engage in actions that support what we have been visualizing or affirming. Take my gardens, for example. The visualizing started back in January by planning what crops to plant and where to plant them. Come spring the action shifted from my head to my hands. There was compost to move, soil to turn, and seeds to plant. Nothing was guaranteed, but without action the plan doesn't get set into motion. It's not so much finishing what I started as it is staying with it through the good (sunshine), bad (drought), and ugly (Japanese beetles) parts. As my mom used to say, "Don't be afraid of a little hard work." Nothing teaches that lesson better than a garden, in my humble opinion!

Picking vegetables as soon as they are ripe often encourages the plant to keep producing. Nature might be hinting at something here. Maybe that's how it works with abundance. You have to be willing to pick an action when the opportunity is ripe. If we make a practice of taking actions that support a thriving life, the Universe responds by bringing in even more prosperity. Every action, no matter how small, lets the Universe know what you're striving for—and it produces big time!

> *"What we plant in the soil of contemplation, we shall reap in the harvest of action."*
> —Meister Eckhart

Full Pocket

I am grateful for all the treasures I found deep in the pockets of my winter barn jacket from last year. Mixed in among the hay chafe: a few edible cough drops—if I don't mind eating a portion of the paper wrapper; a used tissue good for at least two more blows; the gas can cover I thought was lost forever; and Wally fur (eyes filling up with water).

Polished People

The other day I received a bulky package in the mail. As usual, our mailman, Craig, placed it inside our entrance way instead of laying it outside against the door. I could see the struggle in my mind—him trying to hold the door open with the awkward and heavy package obstructing the way through for both of them, and the room that thing must have taken up in his car!

It was in that moment that I "saw" my appreciation for my mailman. To express my gratitude, I left a good helping of my homemade caramels with a Christmas card in the mailbox. I warned him not to eat them frozen for fear of an emergency visit to the dentist. In return we received a very nice thank you and a confession that he didn't wait.

The media would have us believe that we all hate each other. We don't. Appreciation is like polishing people. You shine, they shine, and the whole world gets a little lighter and brighter. Make it from the heart, not obligatory, then you get the warm fuzzy feeling from basking in their glow.

Appreciation polishes people. Polished people shine. Shiny people illuminate the world.

Patch Ponder

It's how I will begin every other day until the harvest ends in August—on my knees next to dew-covered blueberry bushes, filling first my belly then a small bucket with berries. It's a humble, prayerful posture. I seek the plump soft berries that hide among lush green leaves and bowed branches. I take only those ready to relinquish their attachment from tiny stiff stems.

I always come to the patch with an attitude of gratitude. Anyone that helps pick has to be willing. No one is forced to pick because I want the bushes to feel nothing but appreciation for their gift. My movement in the patch is slow and easy. I know I will be returning many more times in the coming weeks. Great care is taken to do no harm or hurt to the bushes that surrender their fruit.

When you pick blueberries, there can be a large cluster, but only a few will have color, and of those few, only one or two will be blue through to the stem. You can feel their ripeness by their willingness to release. I look too, but each year I feel more and look less, or my back yells at me. Blue to the stem are sweet. All others have a tang of sour.

Many of us are working on releasing negative experiences, thoughts, and people. The blueberries reminded me this morning not to force this process. It's OK to wait for the healing to be whole—ripe for the picking. You will be able to release AND relinquish attachment to the experience. There will be a willingness on your part. You will feel it and be OK with wherever the other is in their healing in that shared experience. Only then can you move forward consistently. Healing can hide. Feel for it in a gentle way. You may have to return many more times. Wish you all find the ripe healing in sweetness wherever it's hiding.

Horse-a-holics

To the sound of clip clop and chit chat.
Upon my good Medicine Hat, I sat.
Our noses and toes got a little chilly,
The conversation a little silly,
Spirits uplifted by leaf color and crunch,
I couldn't ask to ride with a better bunch!

The Red Ranger

She's not much to look at on the outside. Bare bones on the inside. Stick shift on the floor. No cruise control, no heated seats, no automatic nothing. On her tailgate are two bumper stickers: I'M A VIETNAM VETERAN and NO FARM-ERS. NO FOOD. What she lacks in appearance appeal is made up in the heart that pounds under her hood.

"She" is a red 1995 Ford Ranger, Reggie White Signature Edition, complete with floor mats bearing the Green Bay Packer "G" emblem. Reggie White played defensive end for the Green Bay Packers football team in the early nineties. He helped the team win Super Bowl XXI with a game-ending sack. Green Bay, Wisconsin, raised his standing in the community to sainthood after that.

I'm borrowing her from my brother, Eddie, while my daughter is home from college during winter break. She was fortunate to have the opportunity to earn money during her time off, but we unfortunately are short on vehicles. Thanks to my brother's generosity, purchasing another vehicle can now be put off until spring.

On the first morning behind the wheel, I spilled most of the coffee in my mug trying to find the cup holder. Its awkward position under the dash and behind the stick shift on the floor created the dilemma. No worries. When I tried to wipe it up, I couldn't even tell where the coffee had spilled. I find it's quite difficult to drink coffee while driving a manual transmission vehicle. Every time I reach for a sip, it seems I have to shift.

Adjectives to describe the complex interior aromas cover a wide range of essences. The prominent odor emanates from the three-inch long, one-inch round cigar stub balanced on the edge of the ashtray. I don't think they put those in vehicles anymore. Do they? I love the scents that swirl around inside an old pickup. The Little Tree air freshener dangling from the rearview mirror is long past its freshening stage. I was a little sad. I wondered what Black Ice X-tra Strength smelled like. My brain is constantly deciphering the potpourri of airborne wonders wafting past my nose. One deep breath in and all those cherished childhood memories bumping around with my dad in his pickup truck were revived.

A two-inch round chip in the windshield, with an uncanny likeness to a bullet hole, lines up squarely between my eyes. Highway speeds give me a palpable feeling of vulnerability as my body slowly slouches down into the well-worn hollow of the seat on the driver's side. Seventy mph seems like I'm exceeding her engine boundaries, so I keep her five miles under the speed limit. Traffic passes me; make that everyone in the slow lane behind me, with an aggressive attitude. I notice their vehicles roll slightly from side to side from the sharp steering maneuver to cut in and out of the lanes at Nascar speeds. "How rude of them," I think to myself. With a quick glance from the passing lane, they think they know where the Red Ranger and I stand in the world. I take her slow and steady daily doses of humility to heart.

I'm going to genuinely miss driving her when Sophie goes back to college at the end of the month. I didn't expect the driving experience to be so fun. Her energy is more zoom zoom then chitty chitty bang bang. She's slowed me down and sharpened my awareness of my surroundings.

Every shift in our lives, up or down, is impeccably timed to slow us down or speed us up. On the winding road of life, free will may be doing the steering but a higher power is working the clutch and stick shift, getting us where we need to be when we need to be there. We are all vehicles of Spirit.

Stick to Kindness

Like a river of sun, the honey pours from the extruder's spigot. I'm preoccupied licking sticky places on my hands and forearms, but I pause to be fully present during this glorious moment overflowing with gratitude.

From a summer of frequent rain came unrelenting blooms. From unrelenting blooms came an abundance of life's sweetness. I taste it in friendship, in a sunrise, in a soft-spoken word of encouragement, in a door held open, in a smile. Kindness sticks sweet to everything it touches. Bee kind.

Hive Haiku

Cold hushes the hive
Darkness dances with the bee
Summer's song is gone.

Summer's Dream

My summer dream is here! The air is heavy with heat, the sun high and still. Endless ribbons of golden light flow through the cloudless sky. In the garden, the green promise of this season's abundance dangles from every vine and stem. An early morning surprise greeted me in the blueberry patch. I popped the plumb blue nuggets in my mouth, bursting the sweet pleasure between my tongue and cheek. Maybe tomorrow a few will make it beyond the patch boundaries to the house—maybe. Having the first crop of hay tucked away in a quiet corner of the shed is the crowning achievement of my hot weather farm duties. Summer's green fills the pockets of my heart with gratitude and contentment. It's a priceless feeling of freedom, knowing you have enough.

This time of sun feeds more than the body. I'll stow away the memories of these soft days to warm my spirit when the landscape turns hard and cold. Summer unfolds life before us, constantly and gracefully, each day a birth of possibility. The dream she has for us is to release our unlimited potential to prosper. May summer's dream awaken and grow within you.

Garden Queen

Summer's youth wanes,
each day riper with fullness,
Phlox's bright eyes open wide.
A delightfully lovely fragrance,
once cradled in her bosomy blooms,
now billows gently in the breeze.
Hot pink petals aflame,
devour the green scenery,
burning off the heat's heaviness.
A sphinx moth visits,
humming above nectar filled flowers,
long tongues dip into wells of sweetness.
The cool of the evening,
invites me back for a visit.
I sit enchanted by the tall aristocratic beauty.
Phlox, you are the queen of my garden empire.
I bow to you.

Ready for Anything

With good reason, many Wisconsinites are agonizing over the blast of Siberia-like cold passing through the region. Temperatures with the wind chill plummeted to fifty degrees below zero in parts of the state last night, creating exasperating problems in our daily existence. We have descended downward to temperatures that could surely freeze hell over.

Dressed in the wool of two sheep, I found myself sweating before I finished feeding and watering the horses. At times, being overprepared can be no better than being underprepared. Sweating was my body's voice of common sense, telling me to restore the balance between the outside and inside climates. Taking two sheep's worth of sweaty wool clothing off was more of a relief than the warmth that consoled me at the wood stove. Extreme cold weighs heavy on the mind and body. Clothing adjustments will be made, a last-minute decision to throw on a pair of ski goggles— borderline genius.

I am grateful for the bitter cold's wide opening to feel compassion's inexhaustible warmth. Folks are filling bird feeders, checking on the elderly, and helping each other—two-legged and four—survive the cold. Duchess, my twenty-three-years-wise Pinto mare, insists on standing outside. Even though I've hung two heat lamps in the shelter and laid down a good two feet of shavings on the floor. I did blanket her, more for my comfort than hers. She spent most of the night standing in the shelter of spruce trees bordering the pasture—out of the wind, underneath the light of stars, in a good two feet of snow. Who am I to argue against twenty-three years of horse sense?

I am also thankful that the jet of glacial cold is forecast to leave the area tomorrow afternoon. By the weekend, meteorologists predict the temperature to be in the upper thirties. Mother Nature's playground is the weather, and she has two pieces of equipment in it—swings and teeter-totters.

I am walking in two winters: one outside and one inside. How well I can balance the climate changes in each has intense implications on my life. Winter invites us to explore the hidden closets in which old thoughts get hung up and forgotten. Temperature fluctuations outside, mood swings inside—both create chaotic conversation within us. We become uncomfortable but they are necessary to "feel" what we're wearing. Adaptability is fundamental to restoring balance in one's life. It is the sheer definition of preparedness—for anything!

Winter Haiku

Winter weans the weak.
Life's circle goes unbroken.
Breath a living prayer.

part six

Medicine Path

Life Is Ceremony

Isn't life ceremony?
Breath it's prayer,
pain and suffering the sacrifice
to grow souls;
love it's healing,
hope it's saving grace,
gratitude the great amplifier of joy.
Every heart a doorway
to the lodge or church or
temple that lives there.
Find your way to a seat; any seat will do.
Sit quietly and listen for a voice.
Even if nothing is heard, something is felt
that makes you better.
All around us medicine; you are medicine.
Not all medicine tastes good,
but it all does some good.
Partake in the communion with nature,
worship the ground you walk on,
have reverence for all life, everywhere.
A beautiful ceremony lives in you.
Bring it to life.
Don't hold on to the gift.
Give it to the world.
You will make missteps along the way,
but the ceremony goes on forever.
It is still happening.

White Prayer

In this, the third week enduring a polar vortex, I retreat from winter's cruel bitter cold, which is a turn toward home, for body and spirit. I joyfully follow the open way to the inner mysteries that warm and sweeten one's soul. A mind's haunting howl is hushed when it's wrapped in winter's white shawl.

The one white that covers the landscape, inside and out, softens the pointy places that poke holes in my peace. Beneath the layers and layers of heavy cold and clothes, I search for something to raise my heart above the worries of this world. I feel the lightness of wonder watching the snowflakes sift and drift through the sky's bluelike dreams in a deep sound sleep. The weather isn't rotten unless you let it spoil your day.

I am blanketed in the warmth of winter's prayer, to trust that Creator will give me strength and endurance to face everything that hurts, everything that makes me turn away, everything that tries to blur the beauty of winter, even a polar vortex.

True Love

At a recent Native American gathering, a mouse tried to join the event. Quick thinking and actions by the person seated by the door prevented its entry. The incident brought to mind a Mouse Spirit message from a previous gathering that was shared with everyone. Mouse Spirit had said, "I no longer want the cheese. I want to be free of the trap." The wisdom is offered with no explanation. It is up to each individual to gain their own understanding.

Lessons can be learned, but the understanding from what we learn leads to knowledge. The knowledge then gives us the natural laws to live by. The teaching walked with and around me for many days. As usual, an understanding came in a quiet moment.

I interpret the baited trap Mouse Spirit speaks of as deception. Many Native American songs reference this. The songs tell us to do it this way, secure our sacred pipes or we may be deceived. In simple terms, the sacred pipe symbolizes a connection to Creator for me. The traps are set when we disconnect from Creator. Through contemplative prayer we can re-establish and deepen that relationship. We begin to learn, understand, know, and live spiritual truths. Within the unconscious of every human being is hidden spiritual truths. Given time and commitment they are revealed to you. Prayer is one method to attain them.

The bait is the powerful illusion of truth in this world that lures us into abandoning our connection to Creator and the spiritual truths that govern all life. At the present time, the illusion of truth is that we hate each other. When we act out from illusion (take the bait), great harm and suffering is created for all those concerned.

Love is the greatest power in the Universe. Not even death can conquer love. It is part of Mouse Spirit's wisdom for me. The world is always trying to build a better mouse trap. Innovation has morphed into revolution. True change will happen when we learn to love those we do not love. An evolution of the soul. It's not coming. It's here.

A heart can only be deceived when it is separated from Creator. Hate trapped in the mind closes the heart to Creator, to love. Hate is a mastermind of traps. It cannot be trusted. If you are unable to reconcile a belief in your mind with an authentic feeling in your heart, it is not true.

As it happened, the day Mouse Spirit's wisdom unfolded, a mouse fell into the horse's grain bin and was trapped. Mouse's liquid black eyes told me to begin living the spiritual truth, to start small. With that, Mouse was taken out to a far field to gather wild food or be food for the wild things. We may be on the cusp of a Universal soul evolution, but it begins small.

Compass

Live water
cradle of life
forever and ever give life
Speak wind
voice of Spirit
quiet the mind's tongue
touch our attention
so we hear your counsel
Reach sun
warm distant souls
turn their faces
to see themselves
Love earth
Mother that carries life
surrounded by your beauty
forgive us
Think mind
of no thoughts
be free
Open heart
close the wounds
of humanity
heal us
Creator
help us remember
how to be a good relative
help us

Seeing Rainbows

Rainbow sightings excite childlike feelings of wonder and awe in me. Intuitively, don't we all recognize the mystical energy rainbows emanate? The bridge between heaven and earth opens before our eyes.

If only people could perceive the facets of our diversity like the millions of water droplets in a rainbow. Reflecting, refracting, and dispersing light, creating a rainbow of humanity by bending our beliefs without breaking them. Something I call compassionate compromise.

Within us a rainbow exists. The seven colors of our chakras correspond to the seven colors of the rainbow. Held within us is also a vessel that holds unimaginable treasures. The riches of the heart can't buy a single thing, but it can connect you to priceless feelings of love. Love is a powerful unifying force. I find it interesting that the "pot of gold" in our internal rainbow isn't at the end but in the middle. Our heart center is the source of a great treasure—compassionate love.

Seeing rainbows gives me hope that one day humanity can bridge the diversity gap with the colors of compassionate compromise. Both ends of a rainbow bend. Where they meet in the middle is the heart of humanity.

Heart Speak Haiku

I see past your words
I feel what you are saying
Hearts speak love's language

Who Am I?

What I am is a short, stocky white women of Polish descent with silver hair. The what is external. Who I am is a strong woman who knows her worth, whose Spirit travels the Red Road with an open heart and mind. The who is internal.

Understanding the distinction between the two can be difficult. The mind only sees the what in our relatives. To know who people are you have to open the eyes in your heart. Those eyes are accepting and compassionate. They give us keen (in)sight.

Vision from this powerful place of perception, where the eyes of our heart and mind see as one, sees through humanness. We begin to appreciate others for whom they are.

Heaven's Home

Our body a house of God, adorned and worshiped.
Behind walls of flesh lies the heart of heaven's home.
Pure love like nature's nakedness feels beauty.
Let love live inside.
Go to the soul's open window.
See what the heart feels.
Of all loves, the greatest is of self.
Beauty is created within the "I" of the heart's home.

Tree Water

There is this sound tree leaves make when autumn winds brush over them with broken, brisk strokes. It happens when leaf edges curl inward like the crest of a wave, the stems in between letting go and hanging on to the branches. If I close my eyes, it doesn't take much imagination to see myself sitting on a sandy beach listening to the motion of the ocean or on the bank of an old river rolling with laughter. I hear the soothing, calm voice of water and instantly my tight thoughts unravel. I call this phenomenon tree water.

Sitting on the porch this morning, the sound of tree water from the little patch of woods in front of our home rushed into my ears and flooded my mind with wonder. Indigenous people teach that water is life, the Peoples' first medicine. For me the meaning of that teaching goes beyond physical wellbeing. Water creates a spiritual thirst for connection, a nonverbal intercommunication of belonging. For many of us, all we need is to hear the healing sound of water to feel the powerful peace of belonging.

The wind stops and I feel merged with Spirit. I am left with this strong desire to participate in life. I belong to something much greater than this world. I am like water, everywhere. Together we heal. Apart we lose heart.

"I believe in God, only I spell it nature."
—Frank Lloyd Wright

All Directions

i
drink sky
eat earth
breathe wind
create light

i
am not the center
but the center is in me
Great Spirit
all around

i
see me
in everything
everything in
me

i
face
all
directions

Hour of a Higher Power

On the cusp of this new season, Mother Earth's breath smells of tender grass, sunlight, and infinite possibility. Oh, the ambitious garden projects spring pushes us to complete in the light of one day! I've learned much about gardening over the years. All that collective wisdom can be summed up in one sentence. Garden chores may stiffen my bones but they soften the soreness in the world.

Divine Hour

There is a Divine power
in the early hours.
The morning star a tiny twinkle,
yet bright enough to make your eyes crinkle.
The hoe's sharp blade breaks the soil's crust
and pulls back a dark moist mound before another thrust.
Pungent earthy smells blow past my nose.
Here is a good home for pea roots to grow.
Sacred seeds of possibility
planted by hands soiled with humility.
Tenderly placed within the prayer of earth's fertile womb
asking for each to bud and bloom.
Oh, the ambitious garden projects spring pushes us to complete!
The sky's daylight is beginning to retreat.
The gardener's body is stiff and bones ache.
Just one more row for goodness' sake!
I rise with Divine power
of the birth hour.
Today's tomorrow,
can't be begged, bought or borrowed.

Cosmic Breath

As I walked toward the frosty field, the crisp freshness of
a mid-November morning burst open inside me. The moist
air's sweetness is so thick that I could taste it on the way in
and out. I momentarily felt suspended in the energetic exchange. I felt the breath give me life. Every breath we take
has that sacred feeling within it. We simply aren't aware of it.

My thoughts wondered—perhaps this breath of air
once crossed the sea or through the needle of a white pine
tree and now me. The wind on its timeless travel through
the eons carries with it the gift of sacred motion and change.
Each breath is an invitation to the Spirits of the elements
to re-establish a relationship with our soul center; to
remember the earth and the stars' lives in us; to remember
life is an exchange, a give and take to remain balanced.

With the next breath, the feeling of aliveness was
gone. I tried to get it back, but my mind got in the way of my
mindfulness. What to do but walk on, and as Mary Oliver
wrote, "Breathe it all in and love it all out."

Wally Walks

Walks with Wally in the open field are unconstrained, his boundary tethered to trust. Obedient to ghostly trails of scent, nothing stops the pursuit except one thing: My booming voice echoing, "BACK!" over the land. He seems to know the precise moment to come in my sights—right before panic could set in. It's the way he returns, his joy knowing no bounds, that makes me believe that love and not fear brought us together.

I often follow him to that place of freedom—flushing out unopened places in my mind; meandering through tight thickets of thought. Like Wally, I go about it unhurried and unworried.

Now that Wally carries the heaviness of age, he's more often than not a few steps behind than a few yards ahead. In his energetic youthful days, he'd pause occasionally to glance back, confirming my pace as either keeping up or falling behind. Adjusting accordingly. I now faithfully return the favor to my dear friend.

Wally's devotion runs as wide and deep as an old river. Together we have walked in beauty, in the darkness that haunts the light, and in each other's souls. Together is all Wally and I have. Our time together is all I will remember. Believe in love and not fear.
Together is all we have.
All of us—together— it's all we have.
Time will remember.

Love Life

Live a life that is loved.
If you're not feeling life's love,
find another way to be living.
A loved life
loves you back.

Share the Road

On a cold, rainy October night I found him, coming home from an extracurricular trip. At the last minute, I swerved to miss what I thought was a crumbled up brown paper bag on the edge of the road. As I passed it, I thought, "Gosh that looked like a kitten. Could it have been a kitten? But it didn't move. Please don't be a kitten."

A short way up the road I turned around and headed back, parking behind the object to see if I could distinguish what it was with my headlights without actually heading out in the rain. It was indeed a kitten, an orange tabby, head drooped down, body close to the pavement. I hurried out of the car to the listless kitten, then slowed, unsure if it would make a run for cover in the ditch. There was no need for fear. The emancipated kitten had little life left. I assumed it had come out onto the road to absorb what it could of the day's heat from the pavement. Gently, I scooped the wet dazed kitten into my warm hands and held it close to my body.

Once in the car, I began delicately drying it off with a blanket from the back seat. Each wipe across its body revealed the severity of the kitten's condition. Every vertebra in its backbone was visible, its skin loose, eyes sunken. In the car's dim interior light, I could tell the kitten could take its last breath at any moment. I couldn't let it die alone. That's when I heard it—the faint sound of a purr. Tears gushed out of my eyes. It must have taken all its strength to purr. That was it; I was going to do all I could to save this one little orange life! Home we sped.

I stayed up with the kitten all night, locked in the bathroom because our then two-year-old yellow lab, Wally, thought it was a chipmunk. I fed it whenever it woke. I was honest with my children about the kitten's condition. My son, teary-eyed, kept telling me to save it. My daughter, a bit older, had no doubts that I'd try my best.

That was eight years ago. We named the male orange tabby Glow because if it wasn't for his "glow" in my headlights, I would have passed him thinking he was a brown paper bag. Glow's feet didn't touch the ground during the first month he was with us. He was my daughter's real life "baby." He was content to be swaddled in her doll blankets, taken for stroller rides around the house, or snuggled up with her in bed. I attribute his strong desire to both give and receive affection to this time of bliss.

Glow left this world unexpectedly on February 15. The road brought him to our family, and it took him from us. Our hearts are heavy with grief. There is a palpable emptiness in my day. His beautiful soul light will be dearly missed. He was my constant companion, a keeper of my heart's secrets, a source of great joy and forever my orange crush. We gave him a good life and he made ours better for it.

Glow was one of those special cats with a personality. He took pleasure from the catnip plants scattered throughout the yard and keeping the rodent population on our farm in check. When you held him, he melted into your body, gently kneading and purring in contentment. He gave abundantly of his love but demanded the same depth of affection be reciprocated whether you felt you had the time or not. He taught our family much about unconditional love, joy's simplicity and the innate ability of playfulness to brighten your spirit.

On the road of life, we pass by many opportunities to show compassion and kindness to other beings. Pay close attention to those that spontaneously place themselves onto your path. They are a special gift. This road of life we are on is meant to be shared. It's the caring we share along the way that makes the reward of our earthly journey real.

The Lakota have a word, Toska, which is said when parting. It is not goodbye. I understand it to mean "I will see you again." Maybe that will be tomorrow, next year, or in the Spirit world—but I will see you again.

Toska Glow. Toska.

part seven

Tiny Teachers

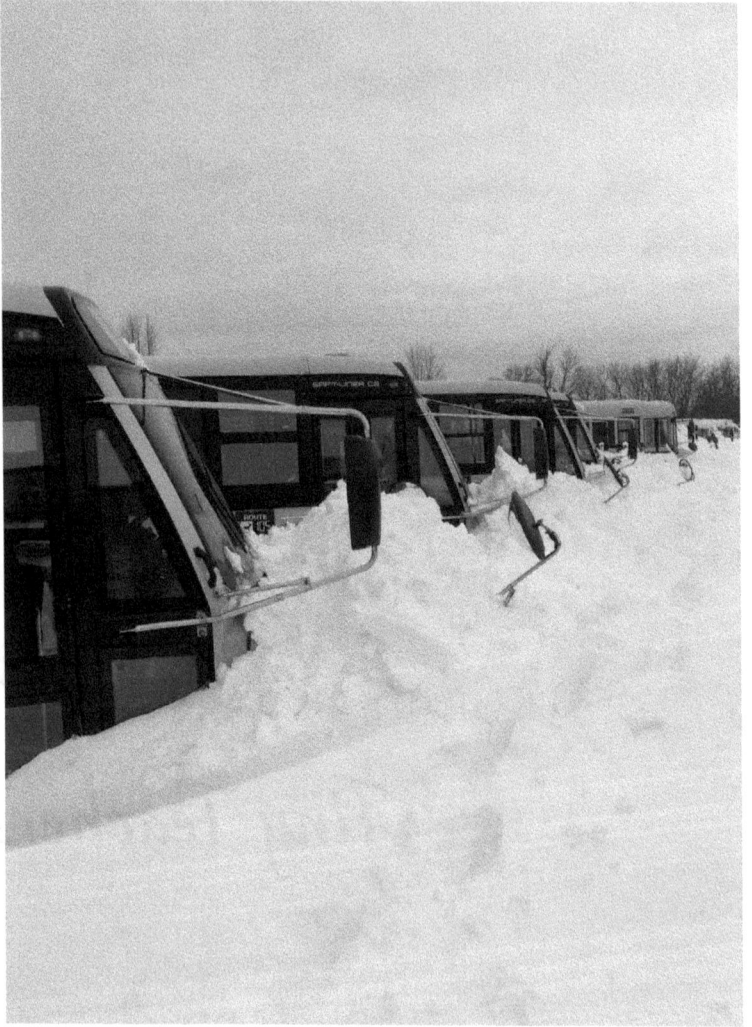

I'm Listening

Child 1: You're not supposed to do that!

Child 2: I'm not listening to you!

Child 1: You have to listen to me! I'm five years old!

Child 2: I don't have to listen to you! (Child 2 is four years old)

Child 1: Actually, I'm five and a half years old.

Child 2: I'm not listening to a five-and-a-half-year-old! Bus driver, how old are you?

Me: I'm fifty-two. Actually, I'm fifty-two-and-a-half years old.

Child 2: I only listen to old people like the bus driver. Humph.

The conversation reminded me of the times I yearned to be old enough for someone—below or above my age—to listen to me.

Now that time has passed and my childhood is far and away, I've learned to choose wisely which voices I allow to influence my decisions. What matters most are not the voices I listen to but the one voice I try to silence. That voice, which is so easily quieted, is the keeper of our deepest knowing about ourselves—our intuition. Whenever we say, "I don't know" or "I can't," we are communicating to our higher self in no uncertain terms with the words "I'm not listening to you!" There is nothing forcing you to listen to your intuition. I wish there was! We've all felt our intuition's silent shouts, "Listen to me!" echoing in our gut at one time or another.

Experience (age) has a way of gaining this understanding. If we could all simply take a breath and feel what we are feeling before tying up our knowing in a "not," there would be no stopping any of us from reaching the unlimited potential untangled in an "I do know" or "I can!" Listen to your gut and you hear your heart.

Do make it an imposition to listen to your intuition.

Stranger to Love

I'm subbing this week for a four-year-old-kindergarten driver while he visits his son out of state. I drove a 4-K route for several years but gave it up last year. My full life overflowed and priorities got shifted. I do love substituting though! Why wouldn't I? Their sweet wisdom gave me enough material for a whole chapter in my book! Little souls possess a superpower to simplify wisdom.

The teacher has been consistent in her strong suggestion to the little ones to make good choices and behave on the bus while the regular driver is absent. I guess they figured the best possible way to insure staying in good graces with the teacher was to compliment me as she observed them loading onto the bus. And compliment me they did! As they filed on, I got complimented on every possible body feature and item of clothing I had on. Not a single flaw, from the gray hair on my head to my unpolished toenails.

"Ms. Angie, I really like your earrings." They were simple silver hoops.

"Ms. Angie, I really really like your hair." My hair was styled by the wind rushing through an open window, most of it no longer contained in a ponytail.

"Ms. Angie, I really really really like your shoes." I'm pretty sure they can't see my feet.

Running out of complimentary options, the tail end of the line started to say, "Ms. Angie, I love you." Aw, the crème de la crème of compliments! Those already seated had to tell me that they loved me too. Tiny voices in a wild stampede shouted out, "I love you!" until the teacher reined them in.

Some might think the "love" was meaningless coming from children I hardly knew, but the gesture touched my heart. The meaning is in the power of the super feeling to lift spirits up, up, and away—together, breaking through the barriers of the mind. I guess you could say love is our superpower. Maybe we just don't fully understand the capabilities of love connection power. Even a stranger. Faster than a speeding bullet! More powerful than a locomotive! Able to leap tall buildings in a single bound! Love connects us for infinity and beyond.

Feel love. Love the feeling. It's hate's kryptonite.

MrsbusdriverladyAngie

Every year the school year begins with a new crop of little ones on my school bus—4Kers. They are four-year-old kindergartners filled with fear, excitement, and every emotion in between. We are into the second week of school here in Wisconsin. I am beginning to see their individual personality's blossom. There is nothing like a new clutch of four-year-olds to teach the virtues of a good sense of humor.

Usually, I tell the little ones to call me, Ms. Angie or Angie. This year I have a sweet little 4K boy who insists on addressing me as MrsbusdriverladyAngie. He is bursting with questions about the ins and outs of riding on a school bus. Unfortunately, I haven't been able to hear them because our conversations go something like this:

4K Boy: Mrsbus . . . driver . . .
Me: Yes?
4K Boy: Mrsbusdriver . . .
Me: Yes?
4K Boy: Mrsbusdriverlady?
Me: What do you need, Hun?
4K Boy: I forgot your name.
Me: Angie
4K Boy: MrsbusdriverladyAngie?
Me: Yes?
4K Boy: I forgot my question.

This conversation repeats every five to ten minutes until we reach the school.

I thought he would tire of the long-winded introduction by now, but he shows no signs of shortening the preface to my name. He is a brightly colored blossom!

It is with great honor and dignity that I have decided to accept the title of MrsbusdriverladyAngie bestowed upon me by a gusty four-year-old. Life is so much easier with a good sense of humor. When life tickles you, don't hold back the laugh.

"A sense of humor is just common-sense dancing."
—William James

Holy Headache

The celebration of Saint Nickolas Day can spin a household and a school bus into a tizzy. The event begins with having to find a place to hang stockings. For those of us without a mantel, it can take repeated reassurances to our little ones that St. Nick can find stockings wherever they are hung.

Then you have to get the much anticipated night of his arrival correct or face self-inflicted parental guilt until Christmas arrives. Is it the night of the 5th or the night of the 6th? Which is it? A quick call to Grandma and she recites the catchy rhyme I can no longer remember and, after a quick check on Google, the day of Saint Nicholas's arrival is confirmed. Heaven help us if St. Nick should come a day early, a day late, or forget us all together. All three scenarios play out in full production on the rolling stage of my school bus in early December.

Children whose houses were visited by the stocking-stuffing saint console friends whose houses were mysteriously missed. When that happens gray vinyl bus seats convert into therapy couches as little minds wrestle with impossible reasons for their misfortune. It's heart wrenching. The crushing blow comes to the empty-stocking children when defiant peers conclude that St. Nick isn't coming to their house at all . . . ever! Quiet sobs and sniffling filter through the bus's chatter. Emotions go amuck.

Eager to show and share what was stuffed into those stockings, therapy sessions end as quickly as they started. Backpacks fly open. Crying subsides. Dollar store trinkets rouse excitement and a clamor of "Let me see! Let me see!" echoes inside the bus. The happy distraction lightens the mood. That is until the last of the cheap Dollar Store trinkets falls and breaks. Crying resumes. But there's still the candy, I say to myself. Maybe it will last until we get to school . . .

By the end of the week, most of Saint Nicholas's gifts have been broken or eaten. The bus settles back into its "As the Wheels Turn" elementary school-age daily drama. Or so I believe.

Then this happens:

Giggles burst above the seat behind me, the infectious kind of laughter that raises curiosity and lowers good intentions. A young voice says, "Now put a mustache on me!" I glance up and ask, "You two aren't drawing mustaches on each other, are you?" Without hesitation the response comes. "Nope. We're playing with our St. Nick stuff." Hmm.

Traffic pulls my attention back to the road. The mustache mystery is on hold for now. As I am about to revisit the mustache mystery, a face pops out from the side of the seat and into the aisle. That little face is trying to catch a glimpse of its reflection in my rearview mirror. Looking up at me is a face covered in what appears to be stamped blue paw prints. Several layers of the stamp cover the child's upper lip. An audible gasp escapes me. My lower jaw drops. My mouth gapes open. OMG! "I thought you told me you weren't drawing mustaches on each other!" Response: "We weren't drawing them. We were stamping them on." St. Nick, you are giving me quite the holy headache. You're really "stocking it to me" this year!

My lesson in all of this? If your life isn't giving you the answer you want, maybe you're asking the question wrong.

God Boss

Conversation on the preschool van I drive:

Little Boy: Bus driver, did you know that Santa works for God?
Me: No, I didn't.
Little Boy: He does! Mom says so. It's because God watches over us . . . everyone . . . EVERYTHING . . . ALL THE TIME! Not just at Christmas like Santa.
Me: Isn't Santa supposed to watch you all year long to know if you've been bad or good?
Little Boy: Yea, but Santa just watches you, not everything. God knows what you're really feeling too.
Me: I guess you could say God created the business (life) . . . lol . . . so that would make him the boss in a way.

I thought this part of our conversation was kind of funny. Since one of the first things that pops out of their four-year-old mouths when another little rider tells them to do something is, "You're not the boss of me!"
Then the wisdom is revealed.

Little Boy: Did you know that when you're sad you can go inside your head and talk to him. God, I mean. Not Santa. It makes you feel better.
Me: I do and it makes me really happy to know that you do too.

As I write this, I can't help but relive the feeling that flushed through me when he spoke his words. I wish you could have felt the feeling in his words, heard the inflection in his voice and the way his speech softened and slowed. You just knew his conversations with God were heart to heart.

Tale of a Tattler

I'm a school bus driver. Our district has a "no eating" rule on the bus. This is mostly to protect those children with food allergies from a medical emergency while they are in transit. It also helps deter bees and wasps from coming onto the bus looking for sweet treats in the garbage.

On one particular day, a kindergartner tattled on a friend for eating candy on the bus. The candy was a large lollipop. I gently asked the little boy to either throw it away or put it back in the wrapper for later. School buses nowadays have high-backed seats, so you can't see anything that is going on in the seats, which makes enforcing the "no eating" policy extremely difficult. I've adapted a strategy of intentional listening (it sounds better than eavesdropping) on conversations that light up my misbehavior radar.

I can hear a quiet exchange of indiscernible words between the tattled on and the tattler. Within a few seconds, the tattler had another tale to tell, "He's still eating his candy, Bus Driver!" I now resort to pleading. "Please, put the candy away. You know eating isn't allowed on the bus."

That's when I hear the rule breaker speak up. In a loud, deliberate voice directed at the tattler he says, "For the last time, I'm not eating. I'm LICKING!"

I can't help but bust into a big smile. Good one! I'm admiring his manipulation skills with a limited vocabulary while at the same time leaving the tattler tongue-tied. Then the pure innocents of the situation revealed a profound truth.

We all know we should talk less and listen more. This experience taught me what we should be listening for—meaning. The meaning given to words is defined by the speaker. If we are not giving our complete attention to listening, talking is meaningless.

Sick Dead and Dying

Before leaving for my van route, I was informed that one of the riders was being driven into school by their mom. At the first stop, I pick up two brothers. Brother 1 immediately asks, "How come Susie isn't on the bus?" Before I could answer, brother 2 asks, "Is she dead?" Me: "NO!" Brother 1: "Is she sick?" Me: "No." Brother 2: "Is she dying"? Me: "No! Her mom is driving her to school today." A few seconds of silence and then both respond, "Oh."

I get to my next pick-up. Before the little girl can get one foot on the bottom step, both of the boys yell out, "The bus driver said Susie is dead!" Brother 1: "No! She's not dead. She's dying!" Brother 2: "She's sick and going to die! Me: "What!?! Hold on, let's start over. Susie is being driven to school today. She's not dead. She's not dying. She's not sick." A few seconds of silence and then Brother 1: "I'm sure glad she's not sick." Those four-year-olds are going to be MY demise!

Kodak Captured

This happens frequently when I'm driving on my morning school bus route. As I head east, I watch in awe as the sun slowly awakens. Brilliant hues of pink, purple, and orange peek over the night's black blanket with blinks of hope and promise for the day ahead. It's difficult sometimes to draw my eyes away from its radiant beauty. My first thought is, "I need to take a picture of this!" I want to remember this beautiful sight and share it with everyone I know! But of course, I can't because I'm driving—a school bus.

I found a better way to capture the moment. I open my heart's lens and let it focus on the beauty before me. In long slow breaths, I inhale the sunrise's hope and promise and drop it into my heart, the one place where the colors will never fade, and at a moment's thought, the beautiful feeling can be retrieved, making every heartbeat a Kodak moment I share with the world.

Every day has pockets of joy-filled wonder. Reach in and take it. A little joy-jing-a-ling-a-ling can change a half-hearted day to wonder full.

About the Author

Born a farmer's daughter, Angeline Haen has a deep love of land and life. She lives close to nature on a small hobby farm with her husband, Andy, in Sobieski, Wisconsin, where wonderment and whimsy come in daily doses. Her grown children, Sophie and Peter, are an infinite source of light, learning, and love. She credits her participation in the Native American community for helping her remember how to be a good relative.

Her first book, *Sweet Wisdoms* (Shanti Arts, 2017), has found its niche as a gift for anyone, any time, or any reason. Her heart is kissed by the delight and joy it continues to share with the world. Shortly after *Sweet Wisdoms* publication, Angeline started a blog by the same name. The blog has been the inspiration for *Sweet Wonder*.

Angeline cheerfully admits to secretly longing to live the life of a hermit. From a young age, she has had a deep love for horses. She cherishes her time in the saddle and the friends that come along for the ride. When she's not wandering with wonder, she can be seen behind the wheel of a school bus or the Oliver 1555 tractor, or at the counter at North Chase Citgo.

SHANTI ARTS

NATURE ▪ ART ▪ SPIRIT

Please visit us online
to browse our entire book catalog,
including poetry collections and fiction,
books on travel, nature, healing, art,
photography, and more.

Also take a look at our highly regarded art
and literary journal, *Still Point Arts Quarterly,*
which may be downloaded for free.

www.shantiarts.com

www.ingramcontent.com/pod-product-compliance
Lightning Source LLC
Chambersburg PA
CBHW070331090426
42733CB00012B/2440